T0194688

An Analysis of

Alfred W. Crosby's

The Columbian Exchange

Biological and Cultural
Consequences of 1492

Joshua Specht
with
Etienne Stockland

Published by Macat International Ltd
24:13 Coda Centre, 189 Munster Road, London SW6 6AW.

Distributed exclusively by Routledge
2 Park Square, Milton Park, Abingdon, Oxon OX14 4RN
711 Third Avenue, New York, NY 10017, USA

Routledge is an imprint of the Taylor & Francis Group, an informa business

www.macat.com
info@macat.com

Cataloguing in Publication Data
A catalogue record for this book is available from the British Library.
Library of Congress Cataloguing-in-Publication Data is available upon request.
Cover illustration: Etienne Gilfillan

ISBN 978-1-912302-47-5 (hardback)
ISBN 978-1-912127-44-3 (paperback)
ISBN 978-1-912281-35-0 (e-book)

Notice
The information in this book is designed to orientate readers of the work under analysis,
to elucidate and contextualise its key ideas and themes, and to aid in the development
of critical thinking skills. It is not meant to be used, nor should it be used, as a
substitute for original thinking or in place of original writing or research. References and
notes are provided for informational purposes and their presence does not constitute
endorsement of the information or opinions therein. This book is presented solely for
educational purposes. It is sold on the understanding that the publisher is not engaged
to provide any scholarly advice. The publisher has made every effort to ensure that
this book is accurate and up-to-date, but makes no warranties or representations with
regard to the completeness or reliability of the information it contains. The information
and the opinions provided herein are not guaranteed or warranted to produce particular
results and may not be suitable for students of every ability. The publisher shall not be
liable for any loss, damage or disruption arising from any errors or omissions, or from
the use of this book, including, but not limited to, special, incidental, consequential or
other damages caused, or alleged to have been caused, directly or indirectly, by the
information contained within.

CONTENTS

THE MACAT LIBRARY

The Macat Library is a series of unique academic explorations of seminal works in the humanities and social sciences – books and papers that have had a significant and widely recognised impact on their disciplines. It has been created to serve as much more than just a summary of what lies between the covers of a great book. It illuminates and explores the influences on, ideas of, and impact of that book. Our goal is to offer a learning resource that encourages critical thinking and fosters a better, deeper understanding of important ideas.

Each publication is divided into three Sections: Influences, Ideas, and Impact. Each Section has four Modules. These explore every important facet of the work, and the responses to it.

This Section-Module structure makes a Macat Library book easy to use, but it has another important feature. Because each Macat book is written to the same format, it is possible (and encouraged!) to cross-reference multiple Macat books along the same lines of inquiry or research. This allows the reader to open up interesting interdisciplinary pathways.

To further aid your reading, lists of glossary terms and people mentioned are included at the end of this book (these are indicated by an asterisk [*] throughout) – as well as a list of works cited.

Macat has worked with the University of Cambridge to identify the elements of critical thinking and understand the ways in which six different skills combine to enable effective thinking.
Three allow us to fully understand a problem; three more give us the tools to solve it. Together, these six skills make up the **PACIER** model of critical thinking. They are:

ANALYSIS – understanding how an argument is built
EVALUATION – exploring the strengths and weaknesses of an argument
INTERPRETATION – understanding issues of meaning

CREATIVE THINKING – coming up with new ideas and fresh connections
PROBLEM-SOLVING – producing strong solutions
REASONING – creating strong arguments

To find out more, visit **WWW.MACAT.COM.**

CRITICAL THINKING AND *THE COLUMBIAN EXCHANGE*

Primary critical thinking skill: CREATIVE THINKING
Secondary critical thinking skill: EVALUATION

One criticism of history is that historians all too often study in isolation, failing to take advantage of models and evidence from scholars in other disciplines. This is not a charge that can be laid at the door of Alfred Crosby. His book *The Columbian Exchange* not only incorporates the results of wide reading in the hard sciences, anthropology and geography, but also stands as one of the foundation stones of the study of environmental history.

In this sense, Crosby's defining work is undoubtedly a fine example of creative thinking. The book comes up with new connections that explain the European success in colonizing the New World more as the product of biological catastrophe (in the shape of the introduction of new diseases) than of the actions of men, and posits that the most important consequences of contact were not political – the establishment of new empires – but cultural and culinary; the population of China tripled, for example, as the result of the introduction of crops from the New World.

Few original hypotheses have proved as stimulating or as influential as the one that Crosby places at the heart of *The Columbian Exchange*.

ABOUT THE AUTHOR OF THE ORIGINAL WORK

Alfred W. Crosby was born in Boston in the United States in 1931 and received his Masters in the art of teaching from the Harvard School of Education and a PhD in history from Boston University. However, he soon became skeptical of the ways in history was taught based on the view that the world became progressively better and that "the good guys always won." These doubts were fostered by a growing personal interest in both environmental matters and political issues of the day, such as the civil rights movement and the Vietnam War. Crosby reinvestigated history and developed new ways of explaining why events happened as they did.

ABOUT THE AUTHORS OF THE ANALYSIS

Etienne Stockland is researching a PhD in environmental history at Columbia University.

ABOUT MACAT

GREAT WORKS FOR CRITICAL THINKING

Macat is focused on making the ideas of the world's great thinkers accessible and comprehensible to everybody, everywhere, in ways that promote the development of enhanced critical thinking skills.

It works with leading academics from the world's top universities to produce new analyses that focus on the ideas and the impact of the most influential works ever written across a wide variety of academic disciplines. Each of the works that sit at the heart of its growing library is an enduring example of great thinking. But by setting them in context – and looking at the influences that shaped their authors, as well as the responses they provoked – Macat encourages readers to look at these classics and game-changers with fresh eyes. Readers learn to think, engage and challenge their ideas, rather than simply accepting them.

'Macat offers an amazing first-of-its-kind tool for interdisciplinary learning and research. Its focus on works that transformed their disciplines and its rigorous approach, drawing on the world's leading experts and educational institutions, opens up a world-class education to anyone.'

Andreas Schleicher
Director for Education and Skills, Organisation for Economic Co-operation and Development

'Macat is taking on some of the major challenges in university education … They have drawn together a strong team of active academics who are producing teaching materials that are novel in the breadth of their approach.'

Prof Lord Broers,
former Vice-Chancellor of the University of Cambridge

'The Macat vision is exceptionally exciting. It focuses upon new modes of learning which analyse and explain seminal texts which have profoundly influenced world thinking and so social and economic development. It promotes the kind of critical thinking which is essential for any society and economy. This is the learning of the future.'

Rt Hon Charles Clarke, former UK Secretary of State for Education

'The Macat analyses provide immediate access to the critical conversation surrounding the books that have shaped their respective discipline, which will make them an invaluable resource to all of those, students and teachers, working in the field.'

Professor William Tronzo, University of California at San Diego

WAYS IN TO THE TEXT

KEY POINTS

- Alfred W. Crosby is an American environmental historian and professor emeritus at the University of Texas at Austin.

- In *The Columbian Exchange*, Crosby argues that the movement of plants, animals, and diseases between Europe and the Americas were the most important legacy of the voyages of the fifteenth-century Italian explorer Christopher Columbus,* considered a key figure in the history of European colonization.

- *The Columbian Exchange* claims that ecological factors were important to the European colonization of the Americas.

Who Is Alfred W. Crosby?

Alfred W. Crosby, the author of *The Columbian Exchange: Biological and Cultural Consequences of 1492* (1972), was born in Boston, Massachusetts, in 1931. He graduated from Harvard University in 1952 before serving in the US Army from 1952 to 1955, stationed in Panama. After the army, he received his Masters in the Art of Teaching from the Harvard School of Education and a PhD in history from Boston University in 1961, working under the direction of Robert E. Moody,* a noted historian of American colonial history. Crosby's dissertation, *America, Russia, Hemp, and Napoleon*, was published in

1965 as his first book; it traced an economic history of the trade between the United States and the Baltic from 1783 to 1812.

Crosby, however, quickly became a critic of the mainstream conventional historical scholarship of his time. His work grew out of the political and intellectual developments of the period; activism based on environmental concerns had been gathering steam since the American biologist Rachel Carson's* influential book *Silent Spring* (1962), which explored the ecological implications of pesticide use. Similarly, Crosby explains in his preface to the 2003 edition that *The Columbian Exchange* emerged from the social upheaval of the 1960s, sparked by America's Civil Rights* and Black Power* movements (key features of the struggle of black Americans for civil and political equality), as well as the Vietnam War* (a conflict in which the United States fought on behalf of South Vietnam against communist North Vietnam at the cost of many thousands of lives).

Previous generations of historians had focused on writing celebratory political histories. In his preface, Crosby observes that "for these men … the good guys always won."[1] But the tumult of the 1960s raised doubts in Crosby's mind about these narratives and he began to consider approaches to history that considered matters beyond the political. This led him to studies in the areas of science and medical anthropology.

During his career, Crosby taught at Ohio State University and Yale. Although he has spent the bulk of his time at the University of Texas at Austin, he wrote and researched *The Columbian Exchange* while at Washington State University. As of 2015, Crosby is professor emeritus of history, geography and American studies at the University of Texas, Austin.

What Does *The Columbian Exchange* Say?

Earlier historians argued that in the period following Christopher Columbus's 1492 voyage from Europe to the Americas (an expedition considered to have vital consequences for European colonialism) history was principally driven by social and political factors. In *The Columbian Exchange*, however, Crosby insists that biological factors were of particular significance to the changes that occurred. He outlines a "Columbian Exchange" in which previously isolated plants, animals, microbes, and peoples came into contact, resulting in a trend towards global biological homogeneity*—in other words, as some plants and animals spread worldwide, their competitors disappeared or were marginalized. In explaining the success of European colonization in the Americas, Crosby speaks of biological shifts, such as the importation of high-calorie foods to Europe, including potatoes, manioc (also known as cassava), and corn.

In considering the demographic* explosion—that is, the increase in population—in Europe in the years following the voyage of 1492, Crosby points to the spread of food crops out of the Americas.[2] He justifies his argument by observing that if you analyze the millions of calories produced per hectare of crop, American plants have a much higher yield than those grown in the Old World* (Africa, Europe, and Asia). Maize (corn), potatoes, and sweet potatoes (yams) all produced more than 7 million calories per hectare, while the only Old World crop to do this was rice, at 7.3 million calories. And manioc, a native plant of South America, produces 9.9 million. These foods became key parts of European and Asian diets, while cassava and maize fueled demographic growth in Africa (where they are now staples). Going in the other direction, Crosby points out that the livestock imported into the Americas enabled the Western hemisphere to support many more people than it had previously. European populations that had grown rapidly—thanks to the spread of New World* crops—would later populate that same New World (that is, the Americas and the islands of the Caribbean) through immigration.

Although earlier works argue that political and technological factors, such as better weapons, drove the Spanish conquest of the

New World, Crosby instead proposes that the devastating spread of the contagious viral disease smallpox* among previously unexposed populations played a more critical role in the submission of New World peoples to the conquistadors* (the Spanish conquerors). Crosby traces the effect of microbial disease on social structure and political organization—and theorizes that epidemics were as devastating indirectly (through economic and social collapse) as directly (through mortality). For example, he argues that the resistance shown by the indigenous Incan people was weakened by a power struggle following the unexpected death of their ruler Huayna Capac,* almost certainly from disease. Crosby also connects this to his larger theme, which stresses the importance of understanding human history in its ecological context. In each chapter of *The Columbian Exchange* he examines a different aspect of history following Columbus's voyage, and shows how biological forces better explain historical phenomena than social and political factors.

Why Does *The Columbian Exchange* Matter?

In its arguments and execution, *The Columbian Exchange* ranks as one of the most important historical works of the past 50 years. Whereas historical writing overwhelmingly revolves around human events and movements, Crosby persuasively argues that the most significant consequences of Christopher Columbus's 1492 voyage were non-human. While this idea is now so widely accepted as to appear obvious, it was revolutionary when the book was first published in 1972.

Furthermore, *The Columbian Exchange* remains unparalleled as an example of how historical inquiry can be conducted by drawing on the sciences. The skill and creativity Crosby showed as he engaged with the scientific literature of the day reveals how much these fields can teach historians—and also proves that historians can contribute important ideas to epidemiology* (the study of the dynamics of epidemics of disease), biology, and other sciences. In consequence,

Crosby's work deserves continued attention both as a significant historical text—foundational in the field of environmental history—and a stellar example of interdisciplinary scholarship (that is, as a work of scholarship that draws on the methods and aims of several fields of inquiry).

It follows that the central ideas of *The Columbian Exchange* have proved enormously influential—starting with the theory that epidemic disease drove the European conquest of the New World. Earlier scholars had explained the conquest as the result of European technology, or the American peoples' "primitive" religious and political systems. But in showing the effects of disease, Crosby undermines these older narratives and demonstrates the importance of biological factors. Crosby's "Columbian exchange" has become an important framework for organizing history into agreed periods. The impact of these ideas, together with their subsequent and lasting influence, have secured the place of Crosby's text among the most significant historical works.

The Columbian Exchange decisively reframed scholars' understanding of Christopher Columbus's 1492 voyage from Europe to the Americas and made a powerful case for the importance of environmental history in all fields of history. On the strength of these accomplishments, the work unlocked entirely new territories of historical inquiry.

NOTES

1   Alfred W. Crosby, *The Columbian Exchange: Biological and Cultural Consequences of 1492* (Westport, CT: Praeger, 2003), xx.

2   Crosby, *The Columbian Exchange*, 165–207.

SECTION 1
INFLUENCES

MODULE 1
THE AUTHOR AND THE HISTORICAL CONTEXT

KEY POINTS

- The American environmental historian Alfred W. Crosby's work demonstrates how non-human actors—plants, animals, and diseases, for example—shape history.

- Crosby became a critic of the "progress narratives" that characterized mainstream historical writing in the mid twentieth-century, according to which the study of history was a question of documenting human progress.

- Crosby wrote *The Columbian Exchange* as the environmentalism movement gathered steam in the 1960s and 1970s.

Why Read This Text?

Alfred W. Crosby's 1972 book *The Columbian Exchange: Biological and Cultural Consequences of 1492* argues that "the most important changes brought on by the Columbian voyages were biological in nature."[1] Crosby examines the implications of contact between the Eastern and Western hemispheres, starting with the voyage made in 1492 by the Italian explorer Christopher Columbus.* Earlier scholarship emphasized how cultural and technological factors shaped the relationships between hemispheres. Crosby contended, however, that non-human factors—among them the exchange of plants, animals, and microbes between the Old* and New Worlds*—mattered more.

Crosby's ideas were shaped by earlier works such as the American historian Walter Prescott Webb's* *The Great Plains* (1931), which began to explore particular environments and ecosystems.[2] Crosby

> ❝ The 1970s was an encouraging period for
> environmentalists, a decade that began in the United
> States with the first Earth Day and the formation of the
> Environmental Protection Agency and that spawned in
> the next few years the Clear Water Act, the Endangered
> Species Act and the Environmental Pesticide Control
> Act. Simultaneously, environmental history emerged as
> a separate and independent school of scholarship. ❞
> Alfred W. Crosby, "The Past and Present of Environmental History"

developed avenues opened in these works to produce a holistic* (that
is, integrated and universal) view of how non-human, biological
factors decisively shape and change human history—as shown in the
aftermath of Columbus's voyage to the New World. While *The
Columbian Exchange* is among several foundational texts in
environmental history, it offers perhaps the most powerful example of
environmental historians reframing popular notions of key historical
moments by drawing both from science and disciplines such as
geography and anthropology.

Author's Life

Crosby received historical training as an undergraduate at Harvard
University and a PhD in 1961 at Boston University under the
direction of the American historian Robert E. Moody.* Despite his
orthodox education, he quickly became a critic of mainstream
historical scholarship. In the 2003 edition of *The Columbian Exchange*,
Crosby described his teachers as men who rarely doubted the basic
goodness of the society for which they had fought in World War II;
they believed the world to be growing progressively better and that
"the good guys always won."[3] But, for Crosby, the tumult of the 1960s
raised doubts about these narratives and he began to consider

approaches to history beyond the political, eventually conducting scholarship in the sciences and medical anthropology. Following a pair of articles in *The American Anthropologist* and the *Hispanic American History Review,* Crosby organized his writings on the consequences of Columbus's voyage into *The Columbian Exchange*. Crosby's teaching career took him to a number of schools—including Ohio State University, Yale, and the University of Helsinki—and he wrote and researched *The Columbian Exchange* during his time at Washington State University. As of 2015, Crosby is professor emeritus of history, geography and American studies at the University of Texas, Austin, where he has spent the bulk of his career.

Author's Background

The political and intellectual climate of the 1960s exerted a profound influence on Crosby's life and work. Environmentalism as a movement had been gaining momentum since the 1962 publication of the American marine biologist Rachel Carson's* book *Silent Spring*, which explored the ecological consequences of pesticide use. The Civil Rights movement* (in the course of which black Americans claimed their rights to equal treatment under the law), the Vietnam War,* and the general tumult of the decade shook his confidence in Western cultural superiority and the idea that history was a question of progress.[4] As a result, Crosby began to look outside the historical profession for solutions to his historical questions. He found his greatest influences in biology and a host of scientific disciplines: anthropology (the study of human cultures), geography, archeology, agronomy (the science of agricultural matters, including soil management), ecology, and other related fields. Acknowledging that the 1960s drove some to dogmatic political positions, he explained simply that "the sixties, which made ideologues of some, drove me to biology."[5]

He also began to study epidemiology* and to probe the importance of disease and food in human history. Once immersed in these subjects, Crosby stopped thinking in terms of the questions that had, until then, driven history as a discipline. As a result, he was free to think about radically different and often bigger issues. For example, Crosby wondered, "what kept people alive long enough to reproduce and what killed them?"[6] Once he began to wrestle with these questions, he saw the decisive influence of non-human factors in human history—and began a quest that would ultimately create an altogether-new lens through which to view historical events.

NOTES

1 Alfred W. Crosby, *The Columbian Exchange: Biological and Cultural Consequences of 1492* (Westport, CT: Praeger, 2003).

2 Walter Prescott Webb, *The Great Plains* (Lincoln: University of Nebraska Press, 1981). For more detail, see Alfred W. Crosby, "The Past and Present of Environmental History," *American Historical Review* 100, no. 4 (1995): 1177–89.

3 Crosby, *The Columbian Exchange*, xx.

4 Crosby, *The Columbian Exchange*, xx–xxi.

5 Crosby, *The Columbian Exchange*, xxi.

6 Crosby, *The Columbian Exchange*, xxi.

ACADEMIC CONTEXT

KEY POINTS

- Alfred W. Crosby turned the attention of historians from politics toward the history of human relationships with the environment.

- Crosby used the tools employed by scientists to determine how human societies survived and perished in the face of environmental pressures.

- Crosby helped bring historians and scientists into a mutual conversation.

The Work in its Context

In 1972, when Alfred W. Crosby published *The Columbian Exchange: Biological and Cultural Consequences of 1492,* his approach to history was revolutionary. Until that point, traditional works focused on the political histories of specific nations. Humans had always stood at the center of historical scholarship; Crosby hoped to change that positioning. To make his case, he argued that a wider set of ecological relationships could decisively shape human history. He formed his theories by examining the non-human factors behind the radical changes that followed the Italian explorer Christopher Columbus's* 1492 voyage from Europe to the Americas.

In adopting this approach, Crosby hoped to solve vexing problems that had plagued earlier historians. Histories of the Spanish conquest* of the New World* focused on Spain's advantages in politics, culture, and technology but failed to account for the rapid decline of the Aztec* and Incan* people of Central and South America. By placing epidemic disease at the center of the story of the Spanish conquest—

> ❝ I fled from ideological interpretations of history and went in search of the basics, life and death … what kept people alive long enough to reproduce, and what killed them? Perhaps food and disease? ❞
>
> Alfred W. Crosby, preface to the 2003 edition of *The Columbian Exchange*

the acute viral disease smallpox* in particular—Crosby fashioned a persuasive and original narrative to explain the scale and speed of the social and political collapse of indigenous American cultures.

Drawing on the aims and methods of several different fields of inquiry, the interdisciplinary nature of *The Columbian Exchange* formed the foundation of Crosby's success and its revolutionary approach. It was so unusual, however, that he had great difficulty in finding a publisher.[1] In the early 1970s, historical works that drew from the social sciences and humanities were far more common, which explains why an idea widely accepted today—that history and the hard sciences have important things to say to each other—was difficult to appreciate when Crosby first published *The Columbian Exchange*. The book went on to play a decisive role in changing this long-standing viewpoint.

Overview of the Field

Crosby's approach had its precursors in the emerging field of environmental history, although his work diverged somewhat in ambition and scope. In 1893, the American historian Frederick Jackson Turner's* seminal paper "The Significance of the Frontier in American History" examined how the American frontier environment helped to promote individualism and democracy. Four decades later, the historian Walter Prescott Webb's* *The Great Plains* (1931) investigated change in particular environments and ecosystems.[2] Although Webb's work was particularly expansive, much of the scholarship that preceded *The Columbian Exchange* was narrowly bounded. Jackson and Webb's works embraced environmental themes more in their general subject matter than in applying sciences such as biology or ecology to spell out human relationships with the non-human world. Crosby certainly drew on these works, widening their approach into a holistic* view of the many ways plant, animal, and microbial factors exert a decisive influence on human history.

To achieve this goal, Crosby sought inspiration from a variety of fields ranging from geography to biology, becoming perhaps the first to bring scholarship in these areas—along with anthropology and epidemiology*—into the fertile ground of historical writing. In doing so, *The Columbian Exchange* raised questions other historians had neglected to ask, and proposed answers they had never considered. In his preface to the 2003 edition, Crosby compared posing the kinds of questions he asked to "replacing the standard film in your camera with infrared or ultraviolet film," concluding that it became possible to "see things you have never seen before."[3]

Academic Influences

With his writing principally influenced by the sciences rather than the historical profession itself, Crosby discovered altogether new vistas. In an article called "The Past and Present of Environmental History" (1995), Crosby cites work in several fields as essential in shaping his thinking and the field of environmental history as a whole. Archeologists were using new techniques to study ancient climates and ecosystems; ecologists such as Frederic E. Clements* and Charles Elton* broadened his views; and geographers such as Paul Vidal de la Blache* were developing theories that were "inspirational to historians with a burgeoning interest in the environment." For example, Vidal de la Blache's theory of possibilism,* with its argument that the environment does not completely decide the nature of human culture and society, replaced crude environmental determinism (according to which the environment does, indeed, determine everything) and pushed historians to examine human societal development within the finite scope of natural environments. Advances in epidemiology also influenced Crosby's work and for Crosby, the willingness of environmental historians to employ the hard sciences—a tendency he greatly shaped—makes the field distinct.

Crosby sums up the revolution: "Environmental historians have discovered that the physical and life sciences can provide quantities of information and theory useful, even vital, to historical investigation and that scientists try and often succeed in expressing themselves clearly."[4]

NOTES

1   Alfred W. Crosby, "Reassessing 1492," *American Quarterly* 41, no. 4 (1989): 661.

2   Walter Prescott Webb, *The Great Plains* (Lincoln: University of Nebraska Press, 1981). For more detail, see Alfred W. Crosby, "The Past and Present of Environmental History," *American Historical Review* 100, no. 4 (1995): 1177–89.

3   Alfred W. Crosby, *The Columbian Exchange: Biological and Cultural Consequences of 1492* (Westport, CT: Praeger, 2003), xxi.

4   Crosby, "The Past and Present of Environmental History," 1189.

MODULE 3
THE PROBLEM

KEY POINTS

- In *The Columbian Exchange*, Alfred W. Crosby sought to account for the "success" of European colonization in the New World.*

- Historians traditionally emphasized superior technology to explain how Europeans conquered Native American populations in the New World.

- Crosby stressed the importance of epidemic diseases as an agent of European colonization.

Core Question

Alfred W. Crosby's core aim, in *The Columbian Exchange: Biological and Cultural Consequences of 1492*, was to decenter the role of human factors in historical scholarship. Indeed, it was his consideration of non-human agents that allowed him to explain how European populations came to grow after Christopher Columbus's* voyage linked the New and the Old Worlds* in 1492. Previous scholarship had suggested urbanization, technological advances, and economic innovations as the key reasons. Crosby concludes that a much more important phenomenon was at work: the spread of higher calorie New World food plants to Europe.

Crosby also demonstrates that the post-1492 trend toward global biological homogeneity* (that is, a decrease in the variety of species) was more significant than the opening of new transatlantic trade routes. As a result of Columbus's voyage, previously separate populations of people, plants, and animals came into contact with each other—and decimated particular populations in the process. Diverse

> ❝ [The] trend towards biological homogeneity is one of the most important aspects of the history of life on this planet since the retreat of the continental glaciers. ❞
>
> Alfred W. Crosby, *The Columbian Exchange*

New World cultures were in part supplanted by imperial* colonial regimes, and the biological diversity of plants and animals gave way to large-scale monocultures (roughly, plantations of single crops) of cotton, sugar, tobacco, and so on. Crosby describes this trend as "one of the most important aspects of the history of life on this planet since the retreat of the continental glaciers."[1]

The Participants

Earlier historians had argued that social and political factors drove history in the period following Christopher Columbus's 1492 voyage. As a notable example, the Belgian historian Charles Verlinden* traced the roots of European imperialism in the New World to Mediterranean history in the Age of the Crusades (the medieval period in which European nations organized military expeditions to the Middle East to "recover" Christian holy sites from Muslims) when "organizational structures and exploitative techniques that would be imposed on America in the sixteenth century were first tried."[2] The French historian Pierre Chaunu* likewise argued that the techniques of political and economic exploitation developed in the sugar islands of the Mediterranean paved the way for colonization in the Americas.

In sharp contrast, however, Crosby maintains in *The Columbian Exchange* that the most significant agents of change were biological. He outlines a "Columbian exchange" in which previously isolated plants, animals, and microbes came into contact with different peoples; the result was an overall trend towards global biological homogeneity. Whereas earlier works cite political and technological factors (including better weapons) as prime drivers in the Spanish conquest of the New World, Crosby proposes something altogether different. The devastating spread of smallpox* to previously unexposed populations, he argues, was more critical in explaining how New World peoples fell to the conquistadors.*

The Contemporary Debate

Crosby's *The Columbian Exchange* was not without its critics. In particular, scholars whose historical narratives stressed the importance of social and cultural factors took issue with the book. As Crosby remarked in his 1987 work *The Columbian Voyages, the Columbian Exchange, and Their Historians*, his approach to European colonization was "recondite [obscure] and discomforting" to those who embraced "Euro-American ethnocentrism"[3] (that is, those whose arguments automatically assumed the primacy of Euro-American perspectives).

One prominent opponent of Crosby's ecological approach was the American economic historian David Landes,* who argued that the "success" of European colonization stemmed from political, social, and cultural factors.[4] The opinions of critics like Landes embraced the importance of technological change—and observed that Columbus's voyage itself depended on social, political, and technological forces that enabled transatlantic travel in the first place. Responses of this kind constitute a key critical analysis of Crosby's work. Although mainstream academic thought has moved towards Crosby's perspective, the critiques of Landes and like-minded historians remain a powerful minority opinion. Environmental historians in subsequent decades, among them the American writers Richard White* and William Cronon,* have likewise argued that Crosby overstates the effect of biological factors on the course of history. While these historians accept the importance of non-human factors, they conclude that such factors are not entirely separate from human culture.

NOTES

1 Alfred W. Crosby, *The Columbian Exchange: Biological and Cultural Consequences of 1492* (Westport, CT: Praeger, 2003), 3.

2 Crosby, *The Columbian Exchange*, 4–5.

3 Alfred W. Crosby, *The Columbian Voyages, the Columbian Exchange, and Their Historians* (Washington, DC: American Historical Association, 1987), 1–2.

4 David S. Landes, *The Wealth and Poverty of Nations: Why Some Are So Rich and Some So Poor* (New York: W.W. Norton, 1998).

MODULE 4
THE AUTHOR'S CONTRIBUTION

KEY POINTS

- In *The Columbian Exchange*, Alfred W. Crosby sought to demonstrate the historical importance of non-human actors such as food crops, animals, and diseases.

- Crosby's focus on ecological factors provided a new way of understanding the success of European colonization* in the New World.*

- In using scholarship from the sciences to shed light on historical questions, Crosby helped to develop a radically new method of studying the past.

Author's Aims

In *The Columbian Exchange: Biological and Cultural Consequences of 1492*, Alfred W. Crosby sought to unite a wide range of scholarship in the humanities, social sciences, and biological sciences, with the goal of proving that "the most important changes brought on by the Columbian voyages were biological in nature."[1] Most if not all previous works emphasized human factors as causing large historical events such as the Spanish conquest of the Aztecs* (the inhabitants of what is today the country of Mexico) or the rapid economic growth of Europe after 1492. Instead, Crosby showed that the critical factors in these processes involved biological shifts—including the importation of new high-calorie foods such as potatoes, manioc, and corn to Europe—or epidemiological* effects, including the spread of smallpox* and other diseases.

Crosby also had a broader intent: to show that the study of non-human environmental factors is essential to the understanding of

> ❝ Virgin soil epidemics are those in which the populations at risk have had no previous contact with the diseases that strike them and are therefore immunologically almost defenseless. The importance of virgin soil epidemics in American history is strongly indicated by evidence that a number of dangerous maladies—smallpox, measles, malaria, yellow fever, and undoubtedly several more— were unknown in the pre-Columbian New World. ❞
>
> Alfred W. Crosby, "Virgin Soil Epidemics as a Factor in the Aboriginal Depopulation in America"

human history. He believed earlier historians had overplayed political and economic elements and so failed to grasp that humans can only be understood when viewed within their ecological context. To clarify this, he outlined how the accidental movement of pathogens* (organisms that cause disease) and other biota (the flora and fauna found in a specific place) could have bolstered the success of European empires in the Americas as much as deliberate human activity. Both materially and conceptually, Crosby hoped to prove that non-human forces act as the major drivers of human history.

Approach
The intellectual framework of *The Columbian Exchange* rests on Crosby's fascination with works in the related fields of anthropology and geography, and in scholarship in the hard sciences: biology, geology, and medicine. Crosby cites the theories of ecologists such as the American scholar of plant evolution Frederic E. Clements* and the English zoologist Charles Elton* as particularly influential; they explored the impact of invasive species on natural ecosystems. His central concept—that the most significant effects of Christopher Columbus's* 1492 voyage to the Americas were biological—grew

from his attempts to synthesize texts from outside history into a single work of historical scholarship.

Crosby built his overarching argument about the centrality of biological factors on several smaller conclusions. In fact, the theme of biology is common to the seemingly disconnected chapters of *The Columbian Exchange*, helping them find their coherence. Each explores one environmental consequence of contact between the hemispheres. This approach is powerful because, even though subsequent scientific research has cast doubt on some of Crosby's claims, he still achieves his overarching goal. Crosby's assertion that the Columbian exchange brought the sexually transmitted disease syphilis* to the Old World* is now disputed, as the balance of evidence indicates the disease probably already existed in Europe. Despite this, a larger, persuasive truth remains intact: when one unites evidence from anthropology, geography, biology, and other fields, non-human factors emerge as the decisive factor behind the changes brought about by the Columbian exchange.

Contribution in Context

Crosby's key themes in *The Columbian Exchange* apply research from the sciences in order to answer specific historical questions. But, to a degree, his aggressive stance on the importance of non-human factors within historical change was inspired by the environmentalist movement, first beginning to develop in the early 1970s. Although this approach would today be quickly identified as environmental history, it did not yet exist as a distinct subfield in 1972, the time that Crosby wrote *The Columbian Exchange*.

It would be incorrect to assume that Crosby's ideas in *The Columbian Exchange* were entirely original. Although he imports pre-existing ideas from the sciences into history, the result still remains highly innovative. The idea that research in the sciences could inform history was novel—especially the politically charged history that surrounded Columbus's 1492 voyage from Europe to the Americas. Furthermore,

Crosby also pushes the reverse: that history can inform the sciences. This notion remains as boundary-shifting today as it was in 1972 because, while historians since have done a good job embracing the social sciences and humanities more broadly, engagement with the hard sciences has been much more limited. Crosby's willingness to draw from biology, medicine, and epidemiology*—the study of epidemics of disease—enabled and empowered him to make ambitious arguments about sweeping historical changes, even as he led sweeping changes in historical study.

NOTES

1   Alfred W. Crosby, *The Columbian Exchange: Biological and Cultural Consequences of 1492* (Westport, CT: Praeger, 2003), xxvi.

SECTION 2
IDEAS

MODULE 5
MAIN IDEAS

KEY POINTS

- The key themes of Alfred W. Crosby's *The Columbian Exchange* are the global spread of pathogens* (organisms that cause diseases) and food crops.

- Crosby's main argument was that the spread of European diseases to the New World* and the importation of New World crops into Europe paved the way for Europe's global hegemony in the centuries after Christopher Columbus's* voyage to the Americas in 1492.

- Crosby structured *The Columbian Exchange* around the spread of specific pathogens, plants, and animals.

Key Themes

Two key themes drive Alfred W. Crosby's *The Columbian Exchange: Biological and Cultural Consequences of 1492*: the global spread of food crops and of epidemic diseases. Within these themes, Crosby examines three distinct factors:

- the migration of diseases between the Old and the New World
- the impact of New World crops on the population of the Old World*
- the results of exchange between hemispheres of animals and non-food plants such as cotton and tobacco.

The Columbian Exchange takes a revolutionary look at the effect of epidemic disease on indigenous populations. Crosby argues that the devastating effects of disease, particularly smallpox,* help explain how Europeans came to dominate the New World. Drawing from his experience as a scholar of Latin America, Crosby recounts the

> **❝** The impact of the smallpox pandemic on the Aztec*
> and Incan empires is easy for the twentieth-century
> reader to underestimate. We have for so long been
> hypnotized by the daring of the conquistador that we
> have overlooked the importance of their biological
> allies. **❞**
>
> Alfred W. Crosby, *The Columbian Exchange*

conquistadors'* rapid conquest of Central and South America. As he explains, "We have for so long been hypnotized by the daring of the conquistador that we have overlooked the importance of their biological allies."[1]

Following his discussion of how microbes impacted the Columbian exchange, Crosby studies the role of plant and animal exchange between the Eastern and Western hemispheres. He maintains that the spread of food crops out of the Americas caused the Old World's population explosion in the years following 1492.[2] Combined, these two overarching themes allow Crosby to outline the specific ways that non-human factors decisively shaped global history after Columbus's voyage from Europe to the Americas that year.

Exploring the Ideas

Crosby traces the effect of microbial disease, making the compelling claim that these affected New World society and politics more than any invasion or military engagement. As Old World diseases moved into the New World, they not only had a direct effect on mortality, indirectly they also caused devastation as they ignited the social and political collapse of native populations. Crosby contends that the Incas,* for example, did not so much yield to the military might of the Spanish as succumb to the diseases they brought with them. The unexpected death of their ruler, Huayna Capac,* almost certainly stemmed from disease and led to chaos and weakness in their attempts to resist the invading armies. Crosby also connects this to his larger theme that human history is shaped by the forces of global ecology.

Crosby reasserts this theme in a subsequent chapter on the sexually transmitted disease syphilis,* which he contends moved from the New World to Europe with devastating effects. While not as disastrous as the smallpox epidemic in the Americas, syphilis had a widespread impact in Europe, and Crosby teases out many cultural ripples in his discussion. Although recent research into the transmission of syphilis suggests Crosby was incorrect in claiming that the disease originated in the New World, his now-disputed argument does not undermine his central theme concerning the spread of diseases through the Columbian exchange.

Crosby also argues that the spread of food crops out of the Americas caused the Old World's post-1492 population explosion.[3] To back up his argument, Crosby bypasses the forces many historians cite— whether in the spheres of politics, conflict, or colonization—and looks instead at the food that crossed from the Americas back to Europe. American plants such as maize (corn), potatoes, and sweet potatoes (yams) all have much denser calorie counts than the crops eaten by Europeans and, in time, these foods became key parts of European and Asian diets. In the opposite direction, livestock imported into the Americas enabled the Western hemisphere to support a burgeoning population of European immigrants. European populations thrived thanks to the spread of New World crops, and became a force of change as they moved into the Americas. Crosby points out, however, that this movement of Old World people would never have taken place if not for the earlier movement of New World crops to their shores.

Language and Expression

In asserting the historical importance of ecological exchanges, Crosby goes beyond food-crop transfers to build his larger argument around the themes of disease and epidemics. He persuades us that non-human factors played a central role in the Columbian exchange by highlighting example after example where plants, animals, or disease drove major changes once attributed to technological change, political superiority, or cultural forces. This structure, which supports his argument well, arises from the stitching together and expansion of two previously published articles.

Crosby's *The Columbian Exchange* addresses traditional historiographical* questions—that is, roughly, questions pertinent to the field of historical research—by using innovative methods. Although Crosby's book would today quickly be identified as a work of environmental history, when he first published *The Columbian Exchange,* this was a field with no distinct identity—arguably, it did not even exist. Thanks to the way he engaged and reframed debates previously explained in political or economic terms, it was a discipline he would help to spawn. In this way, *The Columbian Exchange* provided new answers to familiar questions such as "How did the Europeans conquer the New World?" and "Which factors shaped the rapid economic and demographic* growth of the Old World after 1492?"

The Columbian Exchange also challenged historians to recognize the relevance of knowledge straight from the sciences, forcing them to wade into unfamiliar waters where they would encounter and discover the intellectual currents of archeology, biology, and epidemiology.

NOTES

1   Alfred W. Crosby, *The Columbian Exchange: Biological and Cultural Consequences of 1492* (Westport, CT: Praeger, 2003), 52.

2   Crosby, *The Columbian Exchange*, 52.

3   Crosby, *The Columbian Exchange*, 165–207.

MODULE 6
SECONDARY IDEAS

KEY POINTS

- Alfred W. Crosby examined the intellectual impact of Christopher Columbus's* 1492 voyage to the New World* and presented a pessimistic assessment of the environmental legacy resulting from European conquest.

- In exploring the intellectual impact of the Columbian exchange, Crosby provided subsequent historians with a model to examine the interplay between ideas and the material world.

- Since the publication of *The Columbian Exchange*, historians have acquired a greater understanding of the negative consequences of Columbus's voyage to the Americas.

Other Ideas

One important subordinate idea developed by Alfred W. Crosby in *The Columbian Exchange: Biological and Cultural Consequences of 1492* involves the conceptual effect the Columbian exchange had on intellectual systems on both sides of the Atlantic. In the book's first chapter, "The Contrasts," Crosby explains how the discovery of new peoples, crops, and animals had to be squared with the fundamental beliefs that Europeans and indigenous people held about the world in which they lived. In Spain, for instance, sixteenth-century religious thinkers such as José de Acosta* suggested that multiple creations explained the origins of those native to South America. This is especially interesting because it hints at the relationship between the natural world and the realm of ideas, but it is suggested rather than fully developed.

> 66 Columbus was the advanced scout of catastrophe for Amerindians. There were a few happy sequelae— the flowering of equestrian cultures in the American grasslands, for instance—but on balance, the coming of whites and blacks brought disease, followed by intimidation, eviction, alcoholism ... and obliteration of many peoples and ways of life. 99
>
> Alfred W. Crosby, *The Columbian Voyages, the Columbian Exchange, and Their Historians*

While it is debatable how much Crosby's pessimism pervades his book, it nonetheless represents another important subordinate theme of *The Columbian Exchange*. That it dominates the final essay is quite clear; Crosby closes by telling us that "the Columbian exchange has left us with not a richer but a more impoverished genetic pool. We, all of the life on this planet, are the less for Columbus, and the impoverishment will increase."[1] Crosby's point is that the circulation of peoples, plants, animals, and microbes between the hemispheres created transformations that tended toward biological homogeneity,* squashing human and biological diversity while spreading sameness.

Exploring the Ideas

Crosby's pessimistic assessment is not limited to the book's conclusion; he develops this important sub-theme throughout the text. His claim that "we, all of the life on the planet, are the less for Columbus" was meant to draw attention to the previously neglected ecological and human toll of the explorer's voyages. Crosby contended that increased biological homogeneity and decreased global biodiversity* (the diversity of all the world's many species) represented a key global shift following Columbus's 1492 voyage from Europe to the Americas. Human cultures were threatened or completely eliminated by diseases, just as particular plant and animal populations shrank, disappeared, or expanded—all depending on their role in a newly global economy.

The book's pessimism, which has proved controversial, is counter to perceptions of Columbus as one of history's great heroes. Yet it is fundamental to Crosby's broad point about the importance of non-human factors to the Columbian exchange. The eradication of Amerindian human populations paved the way for the global dominance of European civilization; as Amerindians succumbed to diseases to which they had no natural immunities, it reduced their ability to resist European colonists. As Crosby remarked, "When strangers meet, the degree of difference between their bacterial florae can make more history than the differences between their customs."[2]

Overlooked

While most of *The Columbian Exchange* has been carefully studied, there are nonetheless underappreciated aspects of the text. Perhaps the most neglected part of *The Columbian Exchange* is chapter one, "The Contrasts," in which Crosby weaves a discussion of the differences between the Eastern and Western hemispheres. He tackles this through an examination of "the problem of America"—that is, the effect of Christopher Columbus's "discovery" of the Americas on the European imagination.[3] Though fascinating, this aspect of the text is underdeveloped. As opposed to a thorough analysis, the discussion feels like a series of interesting but disconnected observations about the European imagination. As Crosby wrote, "America was a very square peg to fit into the round hole of Genesis."[4]

Nevertheless, Crosby's investigation of how the New World changed Europeans' ideas about themselves and the environment proved ahead of its time. Though Crosby himself suggests that environmental historians focus too much on material reality and too little on ideas about the environment, his brief discussion in chapter one does consider the world of ideas. Crosby ponders how the "discovery" of the Americas raised questions about Christianity's creation myth, spurring some unorthodox thinkers to conclude that there must have been multiple creations. Rather than merely address the environment itself, Crosby's opening chapter provides insight into ideas of the environment—and how to think about them. This compelling viewpoint reminds us just how much the New World's species and its people impacted on European intellectual and spiritual frameworks, including Christian thought.

NOTES

1   Alfred W. Crosby, *The Columbian Exchange: Biological and Cultural Consequences of 1492* (Westport, CT: Praeger, 2003), 219.

2   Alfred W. Crosby, *The Columbian Voyages, the Columbian Exchange, and Their Historians* (Washington, DC: American Historical Association, 1987), 24.

3   Crosby, *The Columbian Exchange*, 12.

4   Crosby, *The Columbian Exchange*, 12.

MODULE 7
ACHIEVEMENT

KEY POINTS

- "Columbian exchange" has become a phrase in common use by historians and scholars in the social sciences.

- *The Columbian Exchange* was published as environmental historians sought to analyze the relationships between humans and the natural environment.

- Since the 1970s, economists have attempted to measure the impact of the Columbian exchange in quantitative terms—that is, through measurements, including statistics.

Assessing the Argument

Though Alfred W. Crosby's 1972 book *The Columbian Exchange: Biological and Cultural Consequences of 1492* remains as relevant as ever, it has started to appear dated for a curious reason: Crosby's argument has been largely accepted by academics. What was once a revolutionary approach is now common wisdom and environmental historians eagerly engage with scientific research and ecology as they explore humanity's relationship with the environment. While historians and scholars today debate the exact role of epidemic disease in the European conquest, they generally accept Crosby's claim that it holds central importance. Similarly, scholars generally agree with Crosby's claims about the importance of Old World* foods to New World* populations, and the debate has moved on to economists' attempts to quantify them more precisely.[1] Thus the current consensus view holds that Crosby's analysis in *The Columbian Exchange*, while broadly correct, can be pushed further.

> **❝** Crosby's legacy lies not in the comprehensiveness of chronicling the Columbian Exchange, but in the establishment of a perspective, a model for understanding ecological and social events. **❞**
>
> J. R. McNeill, foreword to the 2003 edition of *The Columbian Exchange*

Meanwhile, *The Columbian Exchange* continues to be considered a pioneering work in the field of environmental history. Crosby's approach was so successful that the idea of the "Columbian exchange" now offers a generally accepted framework for making sense of the changes after Christopher Columbus's* 1492 voyage from Europe to the Americas: in fact, scholars freely use the phrase without directly citing Crosby. While many of his specific arguments have lost some relevance because they are so well accepted, his approach remains important and relevant. To quote from the environmental historian J. R. McNeill's* foreword to the 2003 edition of *The Columbian Exchange*, Crosby's legacy "lies not in the comprehensiveness of chronicling the Columbian Exchange, but in the establishment of a perspective, a model for understanding ecological and social events."[2]

Achievement in Context

It is impossible to overstate the novelty of Crosby's argument and methodology when *The Columbian Exchange* was published in 1972. At the time, Crosby's ideas, themes, and methods positioned the book outside mainstream history. Crosby had great difficulty finding a publisher and, when *The Columbian Exchange* finally appeared in print, it could have more appropriately qualified as a work of anthropology or medical history. Yet the book itself, and its eventual percolation throughout the historical realm, has meant that Crosby's ideas now lie at the heart of the field of history. This position would likely have shocked scholars active when the work was first published.

The Columbian Exchange challenged historical writing bound by the cultural and political assumptions prevalent prior to the publication of the text. In criticizing those assumptions, Crosby proposed that universal biological questions held prime importance in driving human history, an approach which served to decenter Eurocentric* narratives that tied the global supremacy of European civilization to its superiority in politics, culture, intellect, and technology. Instead, Crosby revealed that Europe was able to colonize the Americas—and the rest of the world in later centuries—more as a result of an accident of history and a convergence of biological factors.

Limitations

Though the influence of *The Columbian Exchange* outside the historical profession has been limited, the book has produced two important results. First, as we have seen, the Columbian exchange is now the generally accepted framework for thinking about Christopher Columbus's 1492 voyage; and, second, Crosby's emphasis on non-human factors in history has inspired similar approaches in the humanities and social sciences. Scholars in economics, geography, and related fields use the phrase "Columbian exchange" without direct acknowledgement of Crosby's work, a clear sign of the idea's pervasiveness.

Though Crosby's work drew directly from the sciences, and benefited from their impact, it is more difficult to trace the reverse: how it has influenced fields such as biology and epidemiology.* In a sense, those fields were already asking the kinds of questions Crosby hoped to place at the center of historical inquiry. Yet many of the sciences, and especially fields such as public health, have embraced a more historical approach. Thus it is plausible to suggest that Crosby's book might have had an influence.

In the social sciences beyond history, *The Columbian Exchange* has produced a clearer impact. Recent work in economics has tried to quantify the importance and effect of the Columbian exchange on demographic* growth. In an article from the *Journal of Economic Perspectives,* the economics professors Nathan Nunn* and Nancy Qian* note that the study of biological effects from the Columbian exchange has been "neglected" in economics literature, and they provide their own analysis.[3] In their findings, which largely corroborate Crosby's work, they notice important links between New and Old World prices for products that eventually became staples, such as sugar and coffee. Similar work has attempted to quantify the extent of epidemic disease in the New World. Much of this work has tried to add quantitative evidence to Crosby's abstract claims. Indeed, some assessments of Crosby's thinking could change—as happened in the case of his claims about the origin and spread of syphilis.* But, to date, Crosby's arguments have been largely corroborated, and hold sway beyond the field of history.

NOTES

1   Nathan Nunn and Nancy Qian, "The Columbian Exchange: A History of Disease, Food, and Ideas," *Journal of Economic Perspectives* 24, no. 2 (2010): 163–88.

2   J. R. McNeill, foreword to *The Columbian Exchange: Biological and Cultural Consequences of 1492*, by Alfred W. Crosby (Westport, CT: Praeger, 2003), XIII.

3   Nunn and Nancy, "The Columbian Exchange," 164.

MODULE 8
PLACE IN THE AUTHOR'S WORK

KEY POINTS

- The overall thrust of Crosby's work has been to examine how non-human actors (notably plants, animals, and diseases) shaped the course of historical events.

- Alfred W. Crosby's *The Columbian Exchange* set the agenda for his subsequent work.

- *The Columbian Exchange* established Crosby as one of the founding figures of the discipline of environmental history.

Positioning

Alfred W. Crosby's doctoral dissertation *America, Russia, Hemp, and Napoleon* (published as a book in 1965) broached radically different themes to *The Columbian Exchange: Biological and Cultural Consequences of 1492*, examining the politics of trade—particularly in hemp— between Russia and the United States in the years between the American Revolution* and the War of 1812* (both armed conflicts in which the young United States fought Great Britain for its political and economic independence). Although his dissertation was an example of the very kind of political history he would dismiss in future years, glimpses of the later Crosby appear: his subject is large and he traces unexpected connections between disparate places and political events. It would take seven years—and a new decade—before Crosby completed the jump to ecological history.

The Columbian Exchange grew out of two previously published articles, portions of which Crosby used in the book itself. The second chapter, on epidemic disease and Spanish conquest, ran in a journal called the *Hispanic American Historical Review*. Parts of the fourth

> ❝ Twenty years ago I finished a book on the impact of the Columbian voyages on the peoples of the world … I had a hard time finding a publisher, and almost gave up on the book before Greenwood Press spontaneously wrote me to ask if I had anything publishable on hand … the book sold and continues to sell modestly but steadily, three thousand or so a year for a total that must be upwards of forty or fifty thousand by now. ❞
>
> Alfred W. Crosby, "Reassessing 1492"

chapter, on syphilis,* first appeared in *American Anthropologist*. Both articles are largely the same as the book chapters, which helps explain the book's somewhat disconnected structure: six relatively independent essays unite to form Crosby's larger argument. Starting with his exploration of diseases in the aftermath of 1492, Crosby fleshed out *The Columbian Exchange* by attempting to trace all of the effects of Columbus's* voyage—while giving readers a better understanding of the biological causes behind them.

Integration

As Crosby's first significant book publication, *The Columbian Exchange* set the agenda for questions he would explore throughout his career. His subsequent works have examined how humans exist within a broader web of ecological relationships. Following *The Columbian Exchange*, Crosby continued to ask questions that spanned centuries of global change. *Ecological Imperialism: The Biological Expansion of Europe, 900–1900* makes an argument that covers 1,000 years of human history.[1] In this seminal 1986 work, Crosby pursues the argument first developed in *The Columbian Exchange* that it was biology rather than military might that spurred the success of European empires—but dramatically expands the chronological scope. Crosby stretches back to the invasions of Norseman and the Crusades, and examines the making of "Neo-Europes" in the Pacific during the nineteenth century. He also offers a critical examination of the Columbian voyages' historiography* in his short 1987 book *The Columbian Voyages, the Columbian Exchange, and Their Historians*.

Thematically, Crosby's corpus is unified; it analyzes on a large scale the exchange of people, plants, animals, foods, and diseases between hemispheres. He has, however, expanded his geographic scope over the years. In *The Columbian Exchange*, Crosby primarily studies the Americas. In *Ecological Imperialism*, he places the expansion of European disease, animals, and agriculture at the center of global European imperialism.* And his interest in disease, clearly evident in *The Columbian Exchange*, continues in subsequent works such as *America's Forgotten Pandemic*,[2] his influential history of the influenza pandemic of 1918* (a mass outbreak of influenza that infected nearly 500 million people worldwide and killed between 50 and 100 million).[3]

Significance
The Columbian Exchange has been so influential that, in the light of the historical literature that has followed, it is difficult to gauge quite how distinctive and original Crosby's arguments were. Many of Crosby's assertions about the importance of non-human factors in history have turned into fundamental assumptions for mainstream historians.

Although the work stands as one of several foundational texts in environmental history, it also provides perhaps the most powerful example of how environmental historians can reinterpret key historical moments by drawing both from the sciences and from disciplines such as geography and anthropology.

The central ideas of *The Columbian Exchange* have proved influential both in their specific claims and on the greater whole of historical scholarship. The idea, for example, that epidemic disease was the decisive factor in the European conquest of the New World* has been enormously significant. Earlier scholars had put greater weight on European technology and the "primitive" nature of indigenous American religious and political systems as root causes. But, in showing the effects of disease, Crosby undermined these older narratives and bolstered the argument for the importance of non-human factors. Similarly, Crosby's emphasis on a "Columbian exchange" framework resulted in a dominant historical paradigm— that is, a conceptual model—that explained a significant period of history like no previous publication.

The impact created by these ideas on their first appearance, and their subsequent influence in succeeding years, have secured the place of Crosby's text in the list of great historical works.

NOTES

1   Alfred W. Crosby, *Ecological Imperialism: The Biological Expansion of Europe, 900–1900*, 2nd edn (Cambridge: Cambridge University Press, 2004).

2   First published in 1976 as *Epidemic and Peace* by Greenwood Press, Westport, CT.

3   Alfred W. Crosby, *America's Forgotten Pandemic: The Influenza of 1918*, 2nd edn (Cambridge: Cambridge University Press, 2003).

SECTION 3
IMPACT

THE FIRST RESPONSES

KEY POINTS

- Early critics of *The Columbian Exchange* rejected Alfred W. Crosby's claim that biological factors were primarily responsible for the dominance of Western civilization.

- In response to empirical criticism of his work (that is, criticism based on deduction made from observable evidence), Crosby has conceded that syphilis* was not introduced into Europe from the Americas.

- Crosby's work has been supported by a new generation of historians seeking alternative explanations for the global hegemony of European civilizations.

Criticism

The bulk of early criticism directed at Alfred W. Crosby's *The Columbian Exchange: Biological and Cultural Consequences of 1492* addressed the deep pessimism of the book's final essay. "We, all of the life on this planet," he observes, "are the less for Columbus."*[1]

Crosby contended that a key global shift following Christopher Columbus's 1492 voyage from Europe to the Americas was the simultaneous rise in biological homogeneity* and a decline in global biodiversity.* Many reviewers latched onto this claim as overstated and problematic. The geographer Gary S. Dunbar,* professor emeritus at the University of California at Los Angeles, observed that the book "concludes on an unduly pessimistic note."[2] Here one finds the first hints of how Crosby's book stirred up controversy: his assertion that the traditional narratives of European global dominance had been overly celebratory, sidestepping the brutality of European

> 66 Whereas thirty years ago Crosby's ideas met with
> indifference from most historians, neglect from many
> publishers, and hostility from at least some reviewers,
> they now figure prominently in conventional
> presentations of modern history. 99
>
> J. R. McNeill, foreword to the 2003 edition of *The Columbian Exchange*

supremacy. Columbus had (and still has) a national holiday named after him in the United States—and Crosby was telling whoever would listen that Columbus's voyage had made everyone in the world worse off.

This early criticism of Crosby's pessimism foreshadowed the future direction these debates would take. In response to thinkers such as Crosby and the best-selling geographer Jared Diamond,* who tried to explain European dominance as being chiefly the result of non-human factors, many scholars celebrated culture as central to economic and political success. The American economic historian David Landes* challenged Crosby's viewpoint by backing political, social, and cultural factors as key determinants of success or failure.[3] Yet, while the early reception of *The Columbian Exchange* hinted at the debate to come, it would be inaccurate to characterize it as immediately heated. In the early 1970s, scholars had yet to appreciate the full strength of Crosby's argument.

Responses

Crosby's response to criticism of *The Columbian Exchange* is apparent in both the opening of his subsequent book, *Ecological Imperialism* (1986), and his preface to the 2003 edition of *The Columbian Exchange*. Crosby admitted that, in light of new scientific research, he was mistaken about the origin of syphilis and revised his claims as a result. In a sense, this criticism reflected what was special about his book;

because Crosby engaged so thoroughly with scientific research, particular claims merited notice and could be disproved. Crosby also acknowledged, in his 2003 preface, that his account of the ways in which disease epidemics paved the way for European colonization* lacked enough nuance to include non-biological factors. In fact, he had long since produced a more subtle account in a 1976 article "Virgin Soil Epidemics as a Factor in the Aboriginal Depopulation in America."[4]

In other areas, however, Crosby stuck to his guns. He continued to reject the idea that European superiority had more to do with cultural and political organization than non-human factors. In fact, his book *Ecological Imperialism* further attacks this idea. Crosby traces the development of what he calls "neo-Europes" in the New World,* asserting that biological and ecological processes were at the heart of imperialism.* While competing explanations of European dominance in a world marked by the colonialism that followed Columbus's voyage of 1492 remain unresolved, Crosby's approach is the widely accepted account within the historical profession.

Conflict and Consensus

A number of Crosby's empirical conclusions have been revised and rejected, starting with his deduction that the Columbian exchange brought syphilis to Europe. The balance of evidence now indicates that the disease already existed in Europe prior to 1492. Yet the larger point of his work remains persuasive: in combining evidence from anthropology, geography, biology, and other fields, non-human factors emerge as the decisive agents of change brought about by the Columbian exchange.

More recent work accepts the importance of non-human factors (which, for Crosby, means plants, animals, and diseases) while arguing that they cannot be treated as wholly separate from human culture.[5] This literature prefers to blur the boundaries between nature and culture by suggesting how they fundamentally intertwine—a position Crosby hints at but does not directly emphasize in his chapter on epidemic disease and New World conquest. In his article "Virgin Soil Epidemics as a Factor in the Aboriginal Depopulation in America," Crosby explicitly argues that the effects of epidemics are not wholly biological, but must instead be understood as arising from a mix of human and non-human factors.[6]

Within the context of his entire corpus, Crosby's later works serve more to advance his early ideas than directly respond to critics of *The Columbian Exchange*. In fact, Crosby has responded to assessments of *The Columbian Exchange* by incorporating constructive criticisms into his work, while continuing to attack claims for European dominance that focus on the nature of European culture.

NOTES

1   Alfred W. Crosby, *The Columbian Exchange: Biological and Cultural Consequences of 1492* (Westport, CT: Praeger, 2003), 219.

2   G. S. Dunbar, "Review of *The Columbian Exchange*," *William and Mary Quarterly* 30, no. 3 (1973): 543.

3   David S. Landes, *The Wealth and Poverty of Nations: Why Some Are So Rich and Some So Poor* (New York: W.W. Norton, 1998).

4   Alfred W. Crosby, "Virgin Soil Epidemics as a Factor in the Aboriginal Depopulation in America," *William and Mary Quarterly* 33, no. 2 (1976): 289–99.

5   See William Cronon, *Changes in the Land: Indians, Colonists and the Ecology of New England* (New York: Hill and Wang, 1983); and Richard White, *The Roots of Dependency: Subsistence, Environment and Social Change Among the Choctaws, Pawnees and Navajos* (Lincoln: University of Nebraska Press, 1983).

6   Crosby, "Virgin Soil Epidemics," 289–99.

THE EVOLVING DEBATE

KEY POINTS

- Alfred W. Crosby's ecological approach has significantly impacted the historiography* of European colonialism.

- "The Columbian exchange" has become a central concept in environmental history and the history of European imperialism.*

- *The Columbian Exchange* is one of the foundational works of environmental history.

Uses and Problems

Scholars following Alfred W. Crosby have extended his work in important ways. *The Columbian Exchange: Biological and Cultural Consequences of 1492* was a needed corrective since, at the time of publication, historical writing revolved mostly around political or social factors. More recent work has tried to address the interplay between human and non-human aspects, an approach Crosby only hints at in *The Columbian Exchange* but embraces more explicitly in his later writing. In fact, Crosby acknowledges that his emphasis on non-human factors was a starting point for today's scholarship, which tries to break down the boundary between the human and non-human. For example, this literature has agreed that the disease of smallpox* played a decisive role in European conquest—noting, however, that the effects of the smallpox microbe working within a social and political structure made the epidemic deadly. As a result, these works more forcefully claim that all epidemics are produced by biological and cultural factors working in concert.

> ❝ *The Columbian Exchange* has provided economists interested in the long-term effects of history on economics with a rich historical laboratory. Economic studies have thus far mainly focused on how European institutions, through colonialism, were transplanted to non-European parts of the world. ❞
>
> Nathan Nunn and Nancy Qian, "The Columbian Exchange: A History of Disease, Food, and Ideas"

Along these lines, scholars have first and foremost pursued a more nuanced understanding of how biology and humanity feed off each other in a historical framework. Crosby intended *The Columbian Exchange* to serve as a remedy of sorts—he was trying to persuade historians to leave behind their cherished notions of politics and society, and consider the importance of disease and of new types of crops. Although to that end he succeeded, later historians have had to develop stronger theoretical frames of reference. These newer approaches break down divides between nature and culture as arbitrary, and question Crosby's supposition that human and non-human factors can be cleanly separated. However, more theoretically subtle and unified accounts, such as the American environmental historian Richard White's* *The Organic Machine* (1995), would likely not have been possible without Crosby's foundational work.

Schools of Thought

The Columbian Exchange is better known for updating the methods used by historians than inspiring "followers." The historians who established environmental history as a mainstream field during the late 1970s and 1980s—among them, Patricia Limerick,* J. R. McNeill,* Richard White, and Donald Worster*—could not really be described as Crosby's disciples. These historians engaged with themes Crosby addressed and drew from other, older, scholars such as the American environmental historian Walter Prescott Webb.* In that sense, *The Columbian Exchange* proved a key text in a broader trend towards environmental history.

Crosby's perspective is ecological, and this particular approach to history has a number of followers, notably White and the influential environmental historian William Cronon.* Both White's *The Organic Machine*[1] and Cronon's *Changes in the Land* (1983)[2] focus, like *The Columbian Exchange*, on a historical consideration of the ecological relationships—plant, animal, and microbial—enmeshed with human beings and societies. Although the American environmentalist Aldo Leopold* first formulated the idea of writing history ecologically, Crosby was the first academic historian to take up the challenge. Just as Crosby influenced ecological history, he also played a decisive role in encouraging historians to engage with scientific literature.

In Current Scholarship

Crosby's *The Columbian Exchange* decisively reframed the ways in which scholars understood the consequences of Christopher Columbus's* voyage in 1492. His book made a powerful case for the importance of environmental history to all fields of historical inquiry—and, in the process, exerted profound influence on environmental historians. Today, these scholars engage disciplines as diverse as geology and epidemiology,* and the Columbian exchange is now a recognized historical phenomenon. Historians no longer question whether an exchange took place, but try to assess and pinpoint its reach. More recent historical work has sought to better theorize how biological factors and social practices interact, while economists have quantified the extent of the exchange.[3]

Although they may disagree with some of the specifics, today's environmental historians broadly accept the central premises of *The Columbian Exchange*. It would, however, be inaccurate to say that it created a unified school or approach. The work did not seek to create a following of "Crosbians;" rather, it exemplified a specific way of examining history. And this way, with its emphasis on ecological and environmental matters, was already crystallizing when *The Columbian Exchange* was published.

If few of the scholars inspired by the work would consider themselves Crosby disciples, environmental history as a field owes a great deal to him nonetheless—just as it owes a significant debt to earlier scholars and thinkers such as Walter Prescott Webb, Frederick Jackson Turner,* and Aldo Leopold.

NOTES

1   Richard White, *The Organic Machine: The Remaking of the Columbia River* (New York: Hill and Wang, 1995).

2   William Cronon, *Changes in the Land: Indians, Colonists and the Ecology of New England* (New York: Hill and Wang, 1983).

3   Nathan Nunn and Nancy Qian, "The Columbian Exchange: A History of Disease, Food, and Ideas," *Journal of Economic Perspectives* 24, no. 2 (2010): 163–88.

IMPACT AND INFLUENCE TODAY

KEY POINTS

- Alfred W. Crosby's *The Columbian Exchange* is considered a pioneering work in the field of environmental history.

- Crosby's book still poses a challenge to narratives that explain the dominance of Europe in the years following 1492 by pointing to cultural, political, and social factors.

- Opponents of Crosby's approach stress that cultural factors are more critical in explaining European success and power in the early-modern period (roughly, from the end of the fifteenth to the end of the eighteenth century).

Position

The specialized questions raised in Alfred W. Crosby's 1972 work *The Columbian Exchange: Biological and Cultural Consequences of 1492* remain a subject of debate, primarily within the academic world. Although scholars have broadly accepted Crosby's claims, questions about the specific impact of New World* foods or the importance of Old World* disease linger—inspiring both deep inquiry and pointed criticism. While the concept of a Columbian exchange is now an accepted framework for interpreting significant historical features of the last 500 years or so, Crosby's larger point about the importance of non-human factors in explaining European power and its conquest of the Western hemisphere has some notable academic critics.

Although Crosby's argument, once considered revolutionary, broke down paradigms (that is, interpretive models) when it was introduced in the early 1970s, more recent work has challenged his

> ❝ At the time of publication, Crosby's approach to history, through biology, was novel ... Today, *The Columbian Exchange* is considered a founding text in the field of environmental history. ❞
>
> Megan Gambino, "Alfred W. Crosby on the Columbian Exchange"

thesis on theoretical grounds. It has been observed that Crosby treats culture and nature as though historians can consider them separately when, in reality, they are interrelated. Furthermore, it has been contended, Crosby's discussion of the importance of the Columbian exchange on European and American intellectual history is underdeveloped. Recent work has more forcefully emphasized the relationship between ideas and environment. Within the context of environmental history in the twenty-first century, *The Columbian Exchange* is a victim of its own success. It has become so thoroughly incorporated into the study of history that its once-revolutionary ideas seem either clichéd or lacking the nuance of more recent work.

Interaction

Many of the key arguments in *The Columbian Exchange* are now widely accepted and, within the historical profession, Crosby remains little challenged, in part because he has had so much influence on environmental historians. But certain aspects of his thought remain unpopular in various corners of academia. Specifically, these objections concern the implications of Crosby's argument, which implicitly attacks cultural explanations for European global dominance. Suspicion of Crosby's stance has come from conservative academics, and particularly from scholars in fields such as economics. They prioritize the development of European government and financial institutions to explain change in the early-modern period.

The Columbian Exchange has also been criticized as too material, in that it marginalizes the importance of human perceptions and attitudes about the environment. Crosby himself has observed that scholars like him tend "to be more interested in dirt than in perceptions, per se, of dirt. They have no doubts about the reality of what they deal with, nor about their ability to come to grips with it."[1] More recent scholarship contends that this is a significant oversight, since human perceptions of the environment and ecology have served as important forces in human history.

The Continuing Debate

Crosby's move to decenter historical narratives that view the success of European imperialism* as a result of superior technology, society, and politics remains disputed. Though many scholars agree with Crosby, a number of others disagree, particularly in the field of economic history. This disagreement is most obvious when we contrast two recent works by the American geographer Jared Diamond* and the American economic historian David Landes.* In his popular book *Guns, Germs and Steel* (1997), Diamond—an indirect disciple of Crosby—advances an argument quite similar to that proposed in *The Columbian Exchange*. Geography and the natural world, Diamond contends, go a long way towards explaining the success or failure of particular peoples and countries.

Landes, however, in his *The Wealth and Poverty of Nations* (1998), argues that cultural factors are more relevant for explaining European success and power in the early-modern period. Although the weight of scholarship seems to support Crosby and Diamond's side of the debate, in the field of economics a great deal of quantitative scholarship (that is, scholarship drawing on measurable evidence such as statistics) supports Landes's account. Though unpopular with historians, *The Wealth and Poverty of Nations* also enjoys popular support from people who prefer to understand European success as the result of Western cultural values.

While Crosby's academic critics have reasoned arguments in their favor, much of the public conversation is heavily politicized. Crosby himself explains that his work grew out of the turmoil of the 1960s and disillusionment with his conservative predecessors. Generally, defenders of cultural arguments for European dominance are politically conservative, believing in the innate superiority of European civilizations. As the historian Margaret Jacob* has remarked, the very question of the West's success "has become unfashionable on the left … it has been consigned, broadly speaking, to the right."[2] As a result, public conversations on these issues reflect sharp polarization. People on the political left view cultural arguments as Eurocentric* (founded on an unspoken assumption of European superiority) and as justifications for the brutality of colonialism. Meanwhile, right-leaning critics argue that crediting European dominance to nature or chance denies the values that Western democracies hold dear.

The public discourse lacks some level of sophistication, and sharp disagreement divides the two sides on the issue of nature versus culture. But both sides of the academic debate would likely argue that the reality reflects, to some extent, a combination of the two—if they were ever motivated, that is, to hear each other out.

NOTES

1   Alfred W. Crosby, "The Past and Present of Environmental History," *American Historical Review* 100, no. 4 (1995): 1188.

2   Margaret Jacob, "Thinking Unfashionable Thoughts, Asking Unfashionable Questions," *American Historical Review* 105 (2000): 495.

WHERE NEXT?

KEY POINTS

- Alfred W. Crosby's work will remain a foundational text in environmental history.
- The text continues to influence historians who seek to examine the impact non-human actors have had on the course of history.
- The "Columbian exchange" continues to be used as a framework for conceiving of historical periods.

Potential

If Alfred W. Crosby's *The Columbian Exchange: Biological and Cultural Consequences of 1492* must be considered as a foundational text, its continuing relevance, in the sense of its currency, is probably not assured. The ideas Crosby raises and the arguments he advances have had, and will continue to have, an enduring impact on historiography.* Today, chairs are endowed in environmental history and many historians consider the relationship between the human and non-human world. Crosby is in part responsible for this state of affairs.

Yet Crosby's 1972 work was so successful that many of the conversations it provoked have moved far beyond its scope. Crosby's relatively abstract and imprecise arguments about the impact of New World* foods on European population growth have been engaged more directly, with a growing body of work seeking to quantify that impact.[1] Similar conversations are taking place about the relationship between social structure and the course of epidemic disease. Even if the scholarship has moved far beyond *The Columbian Exchange*, one can discern Crosby's influence in each debate and discussion.

> ❝ Thanks to the acceptance of Crosby's work, the term 'Columbian exchange' is now widely used to describe the complex and many-faceted chain of ecological exchanges and impacts that began with Columbus. ❞
>
> Louis De Vorsey, "European Encounters: Discovery and Exploration"

Furthermore, it is likely that, even though *The Columbian Exchange* will eventually be considered to be a text of historical importance rather than a "living" text, it will continue to be relevant to study. Few works since have synthesized such a variety of literatures into a coherent historical argument. In this sense the book is important to subsequent historiography and it can be expected to enjoy an enduring legacy as a masterful example of historical work.

Future Directions

Scholars will continue to develop ideas that Crosby developed and originated. *The Columbian Exchange* discussed the movement of animals and plants between hemispheres, and recent work by Virginia DeJohn Anderson,* a scholar of early-American history, explicitly argues that animals themselves can colonize and that they served as powerful allies in European expansion.[2] While Anderson's work focuses on colonial New England, the importance of animals in the history of colonization as a whole, in different regions of the world, appears to be an important direction for future research. Similarly, the effect of new-crop circulation continues to be hotly debated, and historians and economists will continue to quantify the impact.

The environmental historian J. R. McNeill* has also pushed Crosby's insights in new directions. In the foreword to the 2003 edition of *The Columbian Exchange*, McNeill recalled how the book influenced his thinking as a historian: "My first encounter with the book came on a rainy afternoon in 1982 when I picked it off of a shoulder-high shelf in an office I temporarily occupied. I read it in one gulp neglecting the possibility of supper." McNeill's 2010 book *Mosquito Empires* has applied the approach Crosby forged in *The Columbian Exchange* to provide an ecological answer to a question that has long troubled historians of the Caribbean: why were other Atlantic powers unable to dislodge Spain, a declining power, from the Caribbean in the seventeenth and eighteenth centuries?

Summary

In its arguments and execution, *The Columbian Exchange* stands out as one of the most important historical works of the past 50 years. Crosby persuasively argues that non-human factors caused the most significant consequences of Christopher Columbus's* 1492 voyage from Europe to the Americas. Although this idea is now so widely accepted as to appear patently obvious, it proved revolutionary when the book was first published in 1972. Furthermore, *The Columbian Exchange* remains unparalleled as an example of how historical inquiry might be conducted by drawing from the sciences in an interdisciplinary fashion.

Crosby engaged with scientific literature of the time with consummate skill and creativity, revealing how much these fields can teach historians. In complementary fashion, he also encouraged historians to contribute their ideas to epidemiology,* biology, and the other sciences. As a consequence, Crosby's work deserves continued attention as a foundational text in environmental history and also because it remains one of the best examples of truly interdisciplinary scholarship.

The central ideas of *The Columbian Exchange* have proved to be influential both in their specific claims and in the greater whole. For example, Crosby turned the historical world upside down when he proposed that the decisive factor in European conquest of the New World was the spread of epidemic disease. This marked a significant departure from the work of earlier scholars, who put greater weight on European technology and the American peoples' "primitive" religious and political systems.

In demonstrating the effects of disease, Crosby undermined these older narratives, while simultaneously arguing for the importance of non-human factors such as disease, crops, and animals. Similarly, his emphasis on the framework of a "Columbian exchange" set the stage for the now-dominant paradigm for periodizing history (that is, of conceiving of historical periods). The impact of these ideas at the time of publication, and their subsequent influence in the decades since, secure the place of Crosby's text in the list of great historical works. Much like the crops that fed Europe's population explosion in the post-Columbus years, *The Columbian Exchange* has acted like a seed, growing to nourish a grateful population of historians, scholars, and thinkers.

NOTES

1   Nathan Nunn and Nancy Qian, "The Columbian Exchange: A History of Disease, Food, and Ideas," *Journal of Economic Perspectives* 24, no. 2 (2010): 163–88.

2   Virginia DeJohn Anderson, *Creatures of Empire: How Domestic Animals Transformed Early America* (Oxford: Oxford University Press, 2006).

GLOSSARY

GLOSSARY OF TERMS

American Revolution: a war of independence waged by 13 American colonies against British rule from 1775 to 1783 that resulted in the formation of the United States.

Aztecs: a Native American people founded in about 1100 B.C.E. and first known as inhabitants of the valleys of central Mexico.

Biodiversity: the measure of the variety of species of organisms found on the planet.

Biological homogeneity: a process in which the variety of species in an environment is reduced.

Black Power movement: an American movement that reached prominence in the 1960s and sought to promote the collective interests of African Americans.

Civil Rights movement: a social movement in the United States of the 1950s and 1960s that aimed at abolishing racial discrimination and obtaining civil rights for African Americans.

Colonization: the act of settling in a territory away from one's place of origin and establishing political control there.

Conquistador: a term referring to New World explorers and soldiers of the Spanish Empire. The best-known conquistadors were Hernán Cortés (1485–1547), conqueror of the Aztecs, and Francisco Pizarro (1475–1541), conqueror of the Incan empire.

Demography: the statistical study of human populations using statistics of births, deaths, and diseases.

Epidemiology: the study of the dynamics of disease epidemics.

Eurocentrism: the belief in the cultural exceptionalism and superiority of Euro-American civilizations.

Historiography: the study of methods historians use; the evolution of history as a discipline.

Holistic: an approach that relates to the study of the whole, as opposed to separate parts.

Imperialism: a policy of expanding a country's influence through colonization and military force.

Incas: a pre-Columbian civilization centered in what is now Peru.

Influenza pandemic of 1918: a severe influenza pandemic lasting from January 1918 to December 1920 that infected nearly 500 million people worldwide and killed between 50 and 100 million.

New World: a term originating in the early sixteenth century, referring to the landmasses in the Western hemisphere on which European explorers made landfall.

Old World: the continents of Africa, Europe, and Asia, collectively regarded as the known world prior to European exploration in the Americas in the fifteenth and sixteenth centuries.

Pathogens: an infectious biological agent that causes diseases and illness to a host.

Possibilism: a theory that the environment sets limits, but does not determine, the social and cultural development of human societies.

Smallpox: an infectious disease caused by two viruses, *variola major* and *variola minor*.

Spanish conquest: a process of expansion of the Spanish monarchy into South America that began in 1492 and lasted for three centuries.

Syphilis: a disease transmitted by sexual contact. Its various symptoms include sores on the skin and impaired brain function.

Vietnam War: a protracted conflict (1954–75) in which communist North Vietnam fought against the government of South Vietnam and its principal ally, the United States.

War of 1812: a conflict lasting from 1812 to 1815 between the United States and Great Britain, partly caused by British attempts to restrict US trade.

PEOPLE MENTIONED IN THE TEXT

José de Acosta (1539–1600) was a Spanish Jesuit missionary and naturalist, known for his pioneering work on the natural history of South America.

Virginia DeJohn Anderson (b. 1947) is a professor of early-American history at the University of Colorado, Boulder. She is known for her 2006 book, *Creatures of Empire: How Domestic Animals Transformed Early America*.

Rachel Carson (1907–64) was an American marine biologist and conservationist best known for her 1962 book *Silent Spring*, which explored the environmental effects of pesticide use.

Pierre Chaunu (1923–2009) was a French historian who specialized in Latin American history. He also studied French social and religious history of the sixteenth to eighteenth centuries.

Frederic E. Clements (1874–1945) was an American plant ecologist and pioneer in the study of plant evolution. He is best known for his theory of "climax community," which argues that, after ecological disturbance, vegetation tends naturally towards a mature climax state.

Christopher Columbus (1451–1506) was an Italian explorer who completed four voyages across the Atlantic under the auspices of the Spanish monarchy, and initiated Spanish colonization of the New World.

William Cronon (b. 1954) is a professor of history, geography, and environmental studies at the University of Madison-Wisconsin. He is best known for *Nature's Metropolis: Chicago and the Great West*, winner of the 1992 Bancroft Prize.

Jared Diamond (b. 1937) is a geographer at UCLA, best known for his work *Guns, Germs and Steel* (1997).

Gary S. Dunbar (1931–2015) was an American geographer at UCLA, best known for his work on the disciplinary history of nineteenth- and twentieth-century geography.

Charles Elton (1900–91) was an English zoologist and animal ecologist.

Huayna Capac (1464–1527) was an Incan emperor who died of smallpox following the arrival of the Spanish in South America in the early sixteenth century.

Margaret Jacob (b. 1943) is a distinguished professor of history at UCLA, whose recent work has focused on the cultural origins of the Industrial Revolution.

David Landes (1924–2013) was an American economic historian best known for his work on the Industrial Revolution.

Aldo Leopold (1887–1948) was an American conservationist and advocate for wilderness protection.

Patricia Limerick (b. 1951) is an American environmental historian and one of the leading historians of the American West.

J. R. McNeill (b. 1954) is an environmental historian and historian at Georgetown University, best known for his 2000 book *Something New Under the Sun: An Environmental History of the Twentieth-Century World*.

Robert E. Moody (1901–83) was an American historian who spent the majority of his career at Boston University, specializing in early American history.

Nathan Nunn is a native of Canada and a professor of economics at Harvard University. His work focuses on economic history and developmental economics.

Nancy Qian is an associate professor of economics at Yale University who has worked on the history of famine and economic development.

Frederick Jackson Turner (1861–1932) was an American historian of the early twentieth century best known for his writings on the American frontier.

Charles Verlinden (1907–96) was a Belgian medieval historian who specialized in economic history and the history of colonialism.

Paul Vidal de la Blache (1845–1918) was one of the founders of French geography, best known for his theory of "possibilism," which opposed environmental determinism (that is, it proposed that the environment was not the ultimate decider in the shape of human societies).

Walter Prescott Webb (1888–1963) was an American historian best known for his groundbreaking work on the environmental history of the American West.

Richard White (b. 1947) is an American environmental historian at Stanford University, known for his 1983 work *The Roots of Dependency: Subsistence, Environment and Social Change Among the Choctaws, Pawnees and Navajos.*

Donald Worster (b. 1941) is a distinguished professor of American history at the University of Kansas. One of the founders of environmental history, he is best known for his 1979 book *Dust Bowl: The Southern Plains in the 1930s.*

WORKS CITED

WORKS CITED

Anderson, Virginia DeJohn. *Creatures of Empire: How Domestic Animals Transformed Early America*. Oxford: Oxford University Press, 2006.

Carson, Rachel. *Silent Spring*. New York: Houghton Mifflin, 1962.

Cronon, William. *Changes in the Land: Indians, Colonists and the Ecology of New England*. New York: Hill and Wang, 1983 (revised edn 2003).

Crosby, Alfred W. *America, Russia, Hemp, and Napoleon: American trade with Russia and the Baltic, 1783–1812*. Columbus: Ohio State University Press, 1965.

"Virgin Soil Epidemics as a Factor in the Aboriginal Depopulation in America." *William and Mary Quarterly* 33, no. 2 (1976): 289–99.

The Columbian Voyages, the Columbian Exchange, and Their Historians. Washington, DC: American Historical Association, 1987.

"Reassessing 1492." *American Quarterly* 41, no. 4 (1989): 661–9.

"The Past and Present of Environmental History." *American Historical Review* 100, no. 4 (1995): 1177–89.

America's Forgotten Pandemic: The Influenza of 1918. 2nd edn. Cambridge: Cambridge University Press, 2003.

The Columbian Exchange: Biological and Cultural Consequences of 1492. Westport, CT: Praeger, 2003.

Ecological Imperialism: The Biological Expansion of Europe, 900–1900. 2nd edn. Cambridge: Cambridge University Press, 2004.

Diamond, Jared M. *Guns, Germs and Steel: A Short History of Everybody for the Last 13,000 Years*. New York: Vintage, 1998.

Dunbar, G. S. "Review of *The Columbian Exchange*." *William and Mary Quarterly* 30, no. 3 (1973): 542–3.

Jacob, Margaret. "Thinking Unfashionable Thoughts, Asking Unfashionable Questions." *American Historical Review* 105 (2000): 495.

Landes, David S. *The Wealth and Poverty of Nations: Why Some Are So Rich and Some So Poor*. New York: W.W. Norton, 1998.

McNeill, J. R. Foreword to *The Columbian Exchange: Biological and Cultural Consequences of 1492*, by Alfred W. Crosby. Westport, CT: Praeger, 2003.

Mosquito Empires: Ecology and War in the Greater Caribbean, 1620–1914. Cambridge: Cambridge University Press, 2010.

Nunn, Nathan, and Nancy Qian. "The Columbian Exchange: A History of Disease, Food, and Ideas." *Journal of Economic Perspectives* 24, no. 2 (2010): 163–88.

Turner, Frederick Jackson. "The Significance of the Frontier in American History." In *The Frontier in American History.* New York: Henry Holt, 1921.

Webb, Walter Prescott. *The Great Plains.* Lincoln: University of Nebraska Press, 1981.

White, Richard. *The Roots of Dependency: Subsistence, Environment and Social Change Among the Choctaws, Pawnees and Navajos.* Lincoln: University of Nebraska Press, 1983.

The Organic Machine: The Remaking of the Columbia River. New York: Hill and Wang, 1995.

THE MACAT LIBRARY
BY DISCIPLINE

AFRICANA STUDIES

Chinua Achebe's *An Image of Africa: Racism in Conrad's Heart of Darkness*
W. E. B. Du Bois's *The Souls of Black Folk*
Zora Neale Huston's *Characteristics of Negro Expression*
Martin Luther King Jr's *Why We Can't Wait*
Toni Morrison's *Playing in the Dark: Whiteness in the American Literary Imagination*

ANTHROPOLOGY

Arjun Appadurai's *Modernity at Large: Cultural Dimensions of Globalisation*
Philippe Ariès's *Centuries of Childhood*
Franz Boas's *Race, Language and Culture*
Kim Chan & Renée Mauborgne's *Blue Ocean Strategy*
Jared Diamond's *Guns, Germs & Steel: the Fate of Human Societies*
Jared Diamond's *Collapse: How Societies Choose to Fail or Survive*
E. E. Evans-Pritchard's *Witchcraft, Oracles and Magic Among the Azande*
James Ferguson's *The Anti-Politics Machine*
Clifford Geertz's *The Interpretation of Cultures*
David Graeber's *Debt: the First 5000 Years*
Karen Ho's *Liquidated: An Ethnography of Wall Street*
Geert Hofstede's *Culture's Consequences: Comparing Values, Behaviors, Institutes and Organizations across Nations*
Claude Lévi-Strauss's *Structural Anthropology*
Jay Macleod's *Ain't No Makin' It: Aspirations and Attainment in a Low-Income Neighborhood*
Saba Mahmood's *The Politics of Piety: The Islamic Revival and the Feminist Subject*
Marcel Mauss's *The Gift*

BUSINESS

Jean Lave & Etienne Wenger's *Situated Learning*
Theodore Levitt's *Marketing Myopia*
Burton G. Malkiel's *A Random Walk Down Wall Street*
Douglas McGregor's *The Human Side of Enterprise*
Michael Porter's *Competitive Strategy: Creating and Sustaining Superior Performance*
John Kotter's *Leading Change*
C. K. Prahalad & Gary Hamel's *The Core Competence of the Corporation*

CRIMINOLOGY

Michelle Alexander's *The New Jim Crow: Mass Incarceration in the Age of Colorblindness*
Michael R. Gottfredson & Travis Hirschi's *A General Theory of Crime*
Richard Herrnstein & Charles A. Murray's *The Bell Curve: Intelligence and Class Structure in American Life*
Elizabeth Loftus's *Eyewitness Testimony*
Jay Macleod's *Ain't No Makin' It: Aspirations and Attainment in a Low-Income Neighborhood*
Philip Zimbardo's *The Lucifer Effect*

ECONOMICS

Janet Abu-Lughod's *Before European Hegemony*
Ha-Joon Chang's *Kicking Away the Ladder*
David Brion Davis's *The Problem of Slavery in the Age of Revolution*
Milton Friedman's *The Role of Monetary Policy*
Milton Friedman's *Capitalism and Freedom*
David Graeber's *Debt: the First 5000 Years*
Friedrich Hayek's *The Road to Serfdom*
Karen Ho's *Liquidated: An Ethnography of Wall Street*

The Macat Library By Discipline

John Maynard Keynes's *The General Theory of Employment, Interest and Money*
Charles P. Kindleberger's *Manias, Panics and Crashes*
Robert Lucas's *Why Doesn't Capital Flow from Rich to Poor Countries?*
Burton G. Malkiel's *A Random Walk Down Wall Street*
Thomas Robert Malthus's *An Essay on the Principle of Population*
Karl Marx's *Capital*
Thomas Piketty's *Capital in the Twenty-First Century*
Amartya Sen's *Development as Freedom*
Adam Smith's *The Wealth of Nations*
Nassim Nicholas Taleb's *The Black Swan: The Impact of the Highly Improbable*
Amos Tversky's & Daniel Kahneman's *Judgment under Uncertainty: Heuristics and Biases*
Mahbub Ul Haq's *Reflections on Human Development*
Max Weber's *The Protestant Ethic and the Spirit of Capitalism*

FEMINISM AND GENDER STUDIES

Judith Butler's *Gender Trouble*
Simone De Beauvoir's *The Second Sex*
Michel Foucault's *History of Sexuality*
Betty Friedan's *The Feminine Mystique*
Saba Mahmood's *The Politics of Piety: The Islamic Revival and the Feminist Subjec*t
Joan Wallach Scott's *Gender and the Politics of History*
Mary Wollstonecraft's *A Vindication of the Rights of Woman*
Virginia Woolf's *A Room of One's Own*

GEOGRAPHY

The Brundtland Report's *Our Common Future*
Rachel Carson's *Silent Spring*
Charles Darwin's *On the Origin of Species*
James Ferguson's *The Anti-Politics Machine*
Jane Jacobs's *The Death and Life of Great American Cities*
James Lovelock's *Gaia: A New Look at Life on Earth*
Amartya Sen's *Development as Freedom*
Mathis Wackernagel & William Rees's *Our Ecological Footprint*

HISTORY

Janet Abu-Lughod's *Before European Hegemony*
Benedict Anderson's *Imagined Communities*
Bernard Bailyn's *The Ideological Origins of the American Revolution*
Hanna Batatu's *The Old Social Classes And The Revolutionary Movements Of Iraq*
Christopher Browning's *Ordinary Men: Reserve Police Batallion 101 and the Final Solution in Poland*
Edmund Burke's *Reflections on the Revolution in France*
William Cronon's *Nature's Metropolis: Chicago And The Great West*
Alfred W. Crosby's *The Columbian Exchange*
Hamid Dabashi's *Iran: A People Interrupted*
David Brion Davis's *The Problem of Slavery in the Age of Revolution*
Nathalie Zemon Davis's *The Return of Martin Guerre*
Jared Diamond's *Guns, Germs & Steel: the Fate of Human Societies*
Frank Dikotter's *Mao's Great Famine*
John W Dower's *War Without Mercy: Race And Power In The Pacific War*
W. E. B. Du Bois's *The Souls of Black Folk*
Richard J. Evans's *In Defence of History*
Lucien Febvre's *The Problem of Unbelief in the 16th Century*
Sheila Fitzpatrick's *Everyday Stalinism*

Eric Foner's *Reconstruction: America's Unfinished Revolution, 1863-1877*
Michel Foucault's *Discipline and Punish*
Michel Foucault's *History of Sexuality*
Francis Fukuyama's *The End of History and the Last Man*
John Lewis Gaddis's *We Now Know: Rethinking Cold War History*
Ernest Gellner's *Nations and Nationalism*
Eugene Genovese's *Roll, Jordan, Roll: The World the Slaves Made*
Carlo Ginzburg's *The Night Battles*
Daniel Goldhagen's *Hitler's Willing Executioners*
Jack Goldstone's *Revolution and Rebellion in the Early Modern World*
Antonio Gramsci's *The Prison Notebooks*
Alexander Hamilton, John Jay & James Madison's *The Federalist Papers*
Christopher Hill's *The World Turned Upside Down*
Carole Hillenbrand's *The Crusades: Islamic Perspectives*
Thomas Hobbes's *Leviathan*
Eric Hobsbawm's *The Age Of Revolution*
John A. Hobson's *Imperialism: A Study*
Albert Hourani's *History of the Arab Peoples*
Samuel P. Huntington's *The Clash of Civilizations and the Remaking of World Order*
C. L. R. James's *The Black Jacobins*
Tony Judt's *Postwar: A History of Europe Since 1945*
Ernst Kantorowicz's *The King's Two Bodies: A Study in Medieval Political Theology*
Paul Kennedy's *The Rise and Fall of the Great Powers*
Ian Kershaw's *The "Hitler Myth": Image and Reality in the Third Reich*
John Maynard Keynes's *The General Theory of Employment, Interest and Money*
Charles P. Kindleberger's *Manias, Panics and Crashes*
Martin Luther King Jr's *Why We Can't Wait*
Henry Kissinger's *World Order: Reflections on the Character of Nations and the Course of History*
Thomas Kuhn's *The Structure of Scientific Revolutions*
Georges Lefebvre's *The Coming of the French Revolution*
John Locke's *Two Treatises of Government*
Niccolò Machiavelli's *The Prince*
Thomas Robert Malthus's *An Essay on the Principle of Population*
Mahmood Mamdani's *Citizen and Subject: Contemporary Africa And The Legacy Of Late Colonialism*
Karl Marx's *Capital*
Stanley Milgram's *Obedience to Authority*
John Stuart Mill's *On Liberty*
Thomas Paine's *Common Sense*
Thomas Paine's *Rights of Man*
Geoffrey Parker's *Global Crisis: War, Climate Change and Catastrophe in the Seventeenth Century*
Jonathan Riley-Smith's *The First Crusade and the Idea of Crusading*
Jean-Jacques Rousseau's *The Social Contract*
Joan Wallach Scott's *Gender and the Politics of History*
Theda Skocpol's *States and Social Revolutions*
Adam Smith's *The Wealth of Nations*
Timothy Snyder's *Bloodlands: Europe Between Hitler and Stalin*
Sun Tzu's *The Art of War*
Keith Thomas's *Religion and the Decline of Magic*
Thucydides's *The History of the Peloponnesian War*
Frederick Jackson Turner's *The Significance of the Frontier in American History*
Odd Arne Westad's *The Global Cold War: Third World Interventions And The Making Of Our Times*

The Macat Library By Discipline

LITERATURE

Chinua Achebe's *An Image of Africa: Racism in Conrad's Heart of Darkness*
Roland Barthes's *Mythologies*
Homi K. Bhabha's *The Location of Culture*
Judith Butler's *Gender Trouble*
Simone De Beauvoir's *The Second Sex*
Ferdinand De Saussure's *Course in General Linguistics*
T. S. Eliot's *The Sacred Wood: Essays on Poetry and Criticism*
Zora Neale Huston's *Characteristics of Negro Expression*
Toni Morrison's *Playing in the Dark: Whiteness in the American Literary Imagination*
Edward Said's *Orientalism*
Gayatri Chakravorty Spivak's *Can the Subaltern Speak?*
Mary Wollstonecraft's *A Vindication of the Rights of Women*
Virginia Woolf's *A Room of One's Own*

PHILOSOPHY

Elizabeth Anscombe's *Modern Moral Philosophy*
Hannah Arendt's *The Human Condition*
Aristotle's *Metaphysics*
Aristotle's *Nicomachean Ethics*
Edmund Gettier's *Is Justified True Belief Knowledge?*
Georg Wilhelm Friedrich Hegel's *Phenomenology of Spirit*
David Hume's *Dialogues Concerning Natural Religion*
David Hume's *The Enquiry for Human Understanding*
Immanuel Kant's *Religion within the Boundaries of Mere Reason*
Immanuel Kant's *Critique of Pure Reason*
Søren Kierkegaard's *The Sickness Unto Death*
Søren Kierkegaard's *Fear and Trembling*
C. S. Lewis's *The Abolition of Man*
Alasdair MacIntyre's *After Virtue*
Marcus Aurelius's *Meditations*
Friedrich Nietzsche's *On the Genealogy of Morality*
Friedrich Nietzsche's *Beyond Good and Evil*
Plato's *Republic*
Plato's *Symposium*
Jean-Jacques Rousseau's *The Social Contract*
Gilbert Ryle's *The Concept of Mind*
Baruch Spinoza's *Ethics*
Sun Tzu's *The Art of War*
Ludwig Wittgenstein's *Philosophical Investigations*

POLITICS

Benedict Anderson's *Imagined Communities*
Aristotle's *Politics*
Bernard Bailyn's *The Ideological Origins of the American Revolution*
Edmund Burke's *Reflections on the Revolution in France*
John C. Calhoun's *A Disquisition on Government*
Ha-Joon Chang's *Kicking Away the Ladder*
Hamid Dabashi's *Iran: A People Interrupted*
Hamid Dabashi's *Theology of Discontent: The Ideological Foundation of the Islamic Revolution in Iran*
Robert Dahl's *Democracy and its Critics*
Robert Dahl's *Who Governs?*
David Brion Davis's *The Problem of Slavery in the Age of Revolution*

Alexis De Tocqueville's *Democracy in America*
James Ferguson's *The Anti-Politics Machine*
Frank Dikotter's *Mao's Great Famine*
Sheila Fitzpatrick's *Everyday Stalinism*
Eric Foner's *Reconstruction: America's Unfinished Revolution, 1863-1877*
Milton Friedman's *Capitalism and Freedom*
Francis Fukuyama's *The End of History and the Last Man*
John Lewis Gaddis's *We Now Know: Rethinking Cold War History*
Ernest Gellner's *Nations and Nationalism*
David Graeber's *Debt: the First 5000 Years*
Antonio Gramsci's *The Prison Notebooks*
Alexander Hamilton, John Jay & James Madison's *The Federalist Papers*
Friedrich Hayek's *The Road to Serfdom*
Christopher Hill's *The World Turned Upside Down*
Thomas Hobbes's *Leviathan*
John A. Hobson's *Imperialism: A Study*
Samuel P. Huntington's *The Clash of Civilizations and the Remaking of World Order*
Tony Judt's *Postwar: A History of Europe Since 1945*
David C. Kang's *China Rising: Peace, Power and Order in East Asia*
Paul Kennedy's *The Rise and Fall of Great Powers*
Robert Keohane's *After Hegemony*
Martin Luther King Jr.'s *Why We Can't Wait*
Henry Kissinger's *World Order: Reflections on the Character of Nations and the Course of History*
John Locke's *Two Treatises of Government*
Niccolò Machiavelli's *The Prince*
Thomas Robert Malthus's *An Essay on the Principle of Population*
Mahmood Mamdani's *Citizen and Subject: Contemporary Africa And The Legacy Of Late Colonialism*
Karl Marx's *Capital*
John Stuart Mill's *On Liberty*
John Stuart Mill's *Utilitarianism*
Hans Morgenthau's *Politics Among Nations*
Thomas Paine's *Common Sense*
Thomas Paine's *Rights of Man*
Thomas Piketty's *Capital in the Twenty-First Century*
Robert D. Putman's *Bowling Alone*
John Rawls's *Theory of Justice*
Jean-Jacques Rousseau's *The Social Contract*
Theda Skocpol's *States and Social Revolutions*
Adam Smith's *The Wealth of Nations*
Sun Tzu's *The Art of War*
Henry David Thoreau's *Civil Disobedience*
Thucydides's *The History of the Peloponnesian War*
Kenneth Waltz's *Theory of International Politics*
Max Weber's *Politics as a Vocation*
Odd Arne Westad's *The Global Cold War: Third World Interventions And The Making Of Our Times*

POSTCOLONIAL STUDIES

Roland Barthes's *Mythologies*
Frantz Fanon's *Black Skin, White Masks*
Homi K. Bhabha's *The Location of Culture*
Gustavo Gutiérrez's *A Theology of Liberation*
Edward Said's *Orientalism*
Gayatri Chakravorty Spivak's *Can the Subaltern Speak?*

PSYCHOLOGY

Gordon Allport's *The Nature of Prejudice*
Alan Baddeley & Graham Hitch's *Aggression: A Social Learning Analysis*
Albert Bandura's *Aggression: A Social Learning Analysis*
Leon Festinger's *A Theory of Cognitive Dissonance*
Sigmund Freud's *The Interpretation of Dreams*
Betty Friedan's *The Feminine Mystique*
Michael R. Gottfredson & Travis Hirschi's *A General Theory of Crime*
Eric Hoffer's *The True Believer: Thoughts on the Nature of Mass Movements*
William James's *Principles of Psychology*
Elizabeth Loftus's *Eyewitness Testimony*
A. H. Maslow's *A Theory of Human Motivation*
Stanley Milgram's *Obedience to Authority*
Steven Pinker's *The Better Angels of Our Nature*
Oliver Sacks's *The Man Who Mistook His Wife For a Hat*
Richard Thaler & Cass Sunstein's *Nudge: Improving Decisions About Health, Wealth and Happiness*
Amos Tversky's *Judgment under Uncertainty: Heuristics and Biases*
Philip Zimbardo's *The Lucifer Effect*

SCIENCE

Rachel Carson's *Silent Spring*
William Cronon's *Nature's Metropolis: Chicago And The Great West*
Alfred W. Crosby's *The Columbian Exchange*
Charles Darwin's *On the Origin of Species*
Richard Dawkin's *The Selfish Gene*
Thomas Kuhn's *The Structure of Scientific Revolutions*
Geoffrey Parker's *Global Crisis: War, Climate Change and Catastrophe in the Seventeenth Century*
Mathis Wackernagel & William Rees's *Our Ecological Footprint*

SOCIOLOGY

Michelle Alexander's *The New Jim Crow: Mass Incarceration in the Age of Colorblindness*
Gordon Allport's *The Nature of Prejudice*
Albert Bandura's *Aggression: A Social Learning Analysis*
Hanna Batatu's *The Old Social Classes And The Revolutionary Movements Of Iraq*
Ha-Joon Chang's *Kicking Away the Ladder*
W. E. B. Du Bois's *The Souls of Black Folk*
Émile Durkheim's *On Suicide*
Frantz Fanon's *Black Skin, White Masks*
Frantz Fanon's *The Wretched of the Earth*
Eric Foner's *Reconstruction: America's Unfinished Revolution, 1863-1877*
Eugene Genovese's *Roll, Jordan, Roll: The World the Slaves Made*
Jack Goldstone's *Revolution and Rebellion in the Early Modern World*
Antonio Gramsci's *The Prison Notebooks*
Richard Herrnstein & Charles A Murray's *The Bell Curve: Intelligence and Class Structure in American Life*
Eric Hoffer's *The True Believer: Thoughts on the Nature of Mass Movements*
Jane Jacobs's *The Death and Life of Great American Cities*
Robert Lucas's *Why Doesn't Capital Flow from Rich to Poor Countries?*
Jay Macleod's *Ain't No Makin' It: Aspirations and Attainment in a Low Income Neighborhood*
Elaine May's *Homeward Bound: American Families in the Cold War Era*
Douglas McGregor's *The Human Side of Enterprise*
C. Wright Mills's *The Sociological Imagination*

Thomas Piketty's *Capital in the Twenty-First Century*
Robert D. Putman's *Bowling Alone*
David Riesman's *The Lonely Crowd: A Study of the Changing American Character*
Edward Said's *Orientalism*
Joan Wallach Scott's *Gender and the Politics of History*
Theda Skocpol's *States and Social Revolutions*
Max Weber's *The Protestant Ethic and the Spirit of Capitalism*

THEOLOGY

Augustine's *Confessions*
Benedict's *Rule of St Benedict*
Gustavo Gutiérrez's *A Theology of Liberation*
Carole Hillenbrand's *The Crusades: Islamic Perspectives*
David Hume's *Dialogues Concerning Natural Religion*
Immanuel Kant's *Religion within the Boundaries of Mere Reason*
Ernst Kantorowicz's *The King's Two Bodies: A Study in Medieval Political Theology*
Søren Kierkegaard's *The Sickness Unto Death*
C. S. Lewis's *The Abolition of Man*
Saba Mahmood's *The Politics of Piety: The Islamic Revival and the Feminist Subject*
Baruch Spinoza's *Ethics*
Keith Thomas's *Religion and the Decline of Magic*

COMING SOON

Chris Argyris's *The Individual and the Organisation*
Seyla Benhabib's *The Rights of Others*
Walter Benjamin's *The Work Of Art in the Age of Mechanical Reproduction*
John Berger's *Ways of Seeing*
Pierre Bourdieu's *Outline of a Theory of Practice*
Mary Douglas's *Purity and Danger*
Roland Dworkin's *Taking Rights Seriously*
James G. March's *Exploration and Exploitation in Organisational Learning*
Ikujiro Nonaka's *A Dynamic Theory of Organizational Knowledge Creation*
Griselda Pollock's *Vision and Difference*
Amartya Sen's *Inequality Re-Examined*
Susan Sontag's *On Photography*
Yasser Tabbaa's *The Transformation of Islamic Art*
Ludwig von Mises's *Theory of Money and Credit*

Macat Disciplines

Access the greatest ideas and thinkers across entire disciplines, including

Postcolonial Studies

Roland Barthes's *Mythologies*
Frantz Fanon's *Black Skin, White Masks*
Homi K. Bhabha's *The Location of Culture*
Gustavo Gutiérrez's *A Theology of Liberation*
Edward Said's *Orientalism*
Gayatri Chakravorty Spivak's *Can the Subaltern Speak?*

Macat Disciplines

Access the greatest ideas and thinkers across entire disciplines, including

AFRICANA STUDIES

Chinua Achebe's *An Image of Africa: Racism in Conrad's Heart of Darkness*

W. E. B. Du Bois's *The Souls of Black Folk*

Zora Neale Hurston's *Characteristics of Negro Expression*

Martin Luther King Jr.'s *Why We Can't Wait*

Toni Morrison's *Playing in the Dark: Whiteness in the American Literary Imagination*

Macat analyses are available from all good bookshops and libraries.

Access hundreds of analyses through one, multimedia tool. Join free for one month **library.macat.com**

Macat Disciplines

Access the greatest ideas and thinkers across entire disciplines, including

FEMINISM, GENDER AND QUEER STUDIES

Simone De Beauvoir's
The Second Sex

Michel Foucault's
History of Sexuality

Betty Friedan's
The Feminine Mystique

Saba Mahmood's
*The Politics of Piety:
The Islamic Revival and
the Feminist Subject*

Joan Wallach Scott's
*Gender and the
Politics of History*

Mary Wollstonecraft's
*A Vindication of the
Rights of Woman*

Virginia Woolf's
A Room of One's Own

Judith Butler's
Gender Trouble

 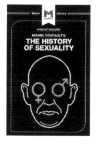  

Macat analyses are available from all good bookshops and libraries.

Access hundreds of analyses through one, multimedia tool.
Join free for one month **library.macat.com**

Macat Disciplines

Access the greatest ideas and thinkers across entire disciplines, including

CRIMINOLOGY

Michelle Alexander's
The New Jim Crow: Mass Incarceration in the Age of Colorblindness

Michael R. Gottfredson & Travis Hirschi's
A General Theory of Crime

Elizabeth Loftus's
Eyewitness Testimony

Richard Herrnstein & Charles A. Murray's
The Bell Curve: Intelligence and Class Structure in American Life

Jay Macleod's
Ain't No Makin' It: Aspirations and Attainment in a Low-Income Neighborhood

Philip Zimbardo's
The Lucifer Effect

Macat analyses are available from all good bookshops and libraries.

Access hundreds of analyses through one, multimedia tool.
Join free for one month **library.macat.com**

Macat Disciplines

Access the greatest ideas and thinkers across entire disciplines, including

INEQUALITY

Ha-Joon Chang's, *Kicking Away the Ladder*

David Graeber's, *Debt: The First 5000 Years*

Robert E. Lucas's, *Why Doesn't Capital Flow from Rich To Poor Countries?*

Thomas Piketty's, *Capital in the Twenty-First Century*

Amartya Sen's, *Inequality Re-Examined*

Mahbub Ul Haq's, *Reflections on Human Development*

Macat Disciplines

Access the greatest ideas and thinkers across entire disciplines, including

GLOBALIZATION

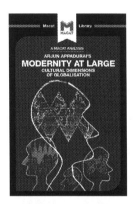

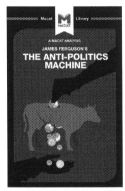

Arjun Appadurai's, *Modernity at Large: Cultural Dimensions of Globalisation*

James Ferguson's, *The Anti-Politics Machine*

Geert Hofstede's, *Culture's Consequences*

Amartya Sen's, *Development as Freedom*

Macat analyses are available from all good bookshops and libraries.

Access hundreds of analyses through one, multimedia tool.
Join free for one month **library.macat.com**

Macat Disciplines

*Access the greatest ideas and thinkers
across entire disciplines, including*

MAN AND THE ENVIRONMENT

The Brundtland Report's, *Our Common Future*
Rachel Carson's, *Silent Spring*
James Lovelock's, *Gaia: A New Look at Life on Earth*
Mathis Wackernagel & William Rees's, *Our Ecological Footprint*

Macat analyses are available from all good bookshops and libraries.

Access hundreds of analyses through one, multimedia tool.
Join free for one month **library.macat.com**

Macat Disciplines

Access the greatest ideas and thinkers across entire disciplines, including

THE FUTURE OF DEMOCRACY

Robert A. Dahl's, *Democracy and Its Critics*
Robert A. Dahl's, *Who Governs?*
Alexis De Toqueville's, *Democracy in America*
Niccolò Machiavelli's, *The Prince*
John Stuart Mill's, *On Liberty*
Robert D. Putnam's, *Bowling Alone*
Jean-Jacques Rousseau's, *The Social Contract*
Henry David Thoreau's, *Civil Disobedience*

Macat Disciplines

Access the greatest ideas and thinkers across entire disciplines, including

TOTALITARIANISM

Sheila Fitzpatrick's, *Everyday Stalinism*
Ian Kershaw's, *The "Hitler Myth"*
Timothy Snyder's, *Bloodlands*

Macat Pairs

Analyse historical and modern issues from opposite sides of an argument. Pairs include:

RACE AND IDENTITY

Zora Neale Hurston's
Characteristics of Negro Expression

Using material collected on anthropological expeditions to the South, Zora Neale Hurston explains how expression in African American culture in the early twentieth century departs from the art of white America. At the time, African American art was often criticized for copying white culture. For Hurston, this criticism misunderstood how art works. European tradition views art as something fixed. But Hurston describes a creative process that is alive, ever-changing, and largely improvisational. She maintains that African American art works through a process called 'mimicry'—where an imitated object or verbal pattern, for example, is reshaped and altered until it becomes something new, novel—and worthy of attention.

Frantz Fanon's
Black Skin, White Masks

Black Skin, White Masks offers a radical analysis of the psychological effects of colonization on the colonized.

Fanon witnessed the effects of colonization first hand both in his birthplace, Martinique, and again later in life when he worked as a psychiatrist in another French colony, Algeria. His text is uncompromising in form and argument. He dissects the dehumanizing effects of colonialism, arguing that it destroys the native sense of identity, forcing people to adapt to an alien set of values—including a core belief that they are inferior. This results in deep psychological trauma.

Fanon's work played a pivotal role in the civil rights movements of the 1960s.

Macat analyses are available from all good bookshops and libraries.

Access hundreds of analyses through one, multimedia tool.
Join free for one month **library.macat.com**

Macat Pairs

Analyse historical and modern issues from opposite sides of an argument. Pairs include:

INTERNATIONAL RELATIONS IN THE 21ST CENTURY

Samuel P. Huntington's
The Clash of Civilisations

In his highly influential 1996 book, Huntington offers a vision of a post-Cold War world in which conflict takes place not between competing ideologies but between cultures. The worst clash, he argues, will be between the Islamic world and the West: the West's arrogance and belief that its culture is a "gift" to the world will come into conflict with Islam's obstinacy and concern that its culture is under attack from a morally decadent "other."

Clash inspired much debate between different political schools of thought. But its greatest impact came in helping define American foreign policy in the wake of the 2001 terrorist attacks in New York and Washington.

Francis Fukuyama's
The End of History and the Last Man

Published in 1992, *The End of History and the Last Man* argues that capitalist democracy is the final destination for all societies. Fukuyama believed democracy triumphed during the Cold War because it lacks the "fundamental contradictions" inherent in communism and satisfies our yearning for freedom and equality. Democracy therefore marks the endpoint in the evolution of ideology, and so the "end of history." There will still be "events," but no fundamental change in ideology.

Printed in the United States
by Baker & Taylor Publisher Services